GUIDO RAHR

Brown Trout Fly Fishing: A Practical Guide

Brown Trout Fly Fishing
A Practical Guide

Chris J. Francis

Illustrated by Tony Amato

Frank
Amato
PORTLAND

DEDICATION

This one is for my parents, Dan and Jill. I have incurred a debt which can never be repaid.

ACKNOWLEDGMENTS

When I guided in Alaska, we (all the guides) would help each other out by trading amongst ourselves, flies, tippet material, rods, wader sealant, days off, and anything else which was necessary for daily operations. This became known as stream debt and we managed to keep a fairly accurate mental ledger. Stream debt, always its own entity, was never allowed to be consolidated with any other kinds of debt (like beer debt) and (unlike beer debt) never involved any money changing hands. Strictly a hard goods and services exchange.

During the writing of this book I am afraid I have discovered yet another type of debt—book debt. While I am pretty sure I do not owe anyone money, the favors seemed to pile up at a pretty quick rate. I'm worried I may not have enough spare flies and extra tippet to go around this time. As a compromise I offer the following people my heartfelt thanks.

Steve Bodio for trying to teach a fly fishing guide to write. I'm sure by now he thinks a career as a rodeo bull rider would have been easier. I remain awed by his talent with the written word.

My sister, Nicole Francis, for helping me access the New York City Public Library.

Dr. J.M. Conley has influenced my thinking more than any other. What else can I say? Fly fisherman, tier, and friend extraordinaire. May our increasingly busy schedules always have time for all three.

Dave Kumlien at Montana Troutfitter's Orvis Shop generously gave me fly shop work during the winter months even though, I suspect, he really didn't need the help. George Cook at Sage Rods along with Ron Foster and Mike Harrington of Hodgman Waders have always understood a guide's budget does not always correspond with owning the best equipment. Dave Egdorf at Western Alaska Sportfishing and Dan and Randy Busch of Kodiak Island River Camps have been very good to me over the years. Both outfits have always offered work when I needed it.

Ted Turner, Jane Fonda, Beau Turner and the rest of their family for needing a stream keeper year-round. Their support has been unequaled.

David Freeman, Blake Larue, Dale Sexton and Fred Kratz for their friendship. This bunch of outlaws now stretches from Pakistan to Montana, via Alaska's bush, and includes one M.I.A. (Fred, if you happen to read this, "Ollie-Ollie-Oxen-Free!" The time has passed.) I'm sure a person could guide and fish with a saner crowd, but it never crossed my mind.

Dorothy Heacox and Wayne Trimm graciously allowed me to reproduce two charts from Wayne and Cecil's book *The Complete Brown Trout*. Venice Beske helped me find many of the old books needed to write about the history of the brown trout. I seriously doubt anyone knows our nation's library systems better. Dick Stewart gave me permission to use the fly recipe format from he and Farrow Allen's book. Their recipe format should become "the standard."

Christie, Kindra, and Graham, my family, for their unselfish support.

And finally, thanks to Frank and Nick Amato for their early and continued support, and for being publishers who are not afraid to enter a dark horse in the race.

Chris J. Francis
March, 1996
Gallatin Gateway, MT

Frank Amato Publications, Inc., P.O. Box 82112, Portland, Oregon 97282
503•653•8108
Photos for Front and Back Cover and Border Design: Guido Rahr
All photos by the author except where otherwise noted
Illustrations by Tony Amato
Book and Cover Design: Kathy Johnson
Printed in Hong Kong

UPC Hardbound: 0-66066-00256-3   Softbound: 0-66066-00255-6
ISBN Hardbound: 1-57188-064-X   Softbound: 1-57188-063-1
1 3 5 7 9 10 8 6 4 2

CONTENTS

INTRODUCTION

I fished Montana for six years before I caught my first trout over 20 inches. It was a brown trout. I was fishing a large Woolly Bugger on a very cold July day. My technique for fishing was to cast a large streamer into the bank, strip it out and hope that a fish would go for it. When the fish struck the streamer and I set the hook there was absolutely no movement in the line. I began to doubt whether or not I had hooked a fish or a submerged log. Wisely I decided to wait before trying to play the fish. After several minutes the line began to move. Luckily, my guide coached me on how to handle the fish and land it. Since that time I have been an avid brown trout fisherman and I have caught a number of brown trout, however none of them have been over 20 inches.

After reading the manuscript for Chris Francis' new book, *Brown Trout Fly Fishing: A Practical Guide*, I began to understand why I've not had much success on large browns. I, like many other fishermen, have never regarded, or fished for, brown trout any differently than other species of trout. I didn't understand the habits and nature of the fish, nor did I know where to look for them in streams or lakes. My fishing skills also left a great deal to be desired.

Chris Francis is a hard-core brown trout fly fisherman. He has spent years studying and fishing for brown trout specifically. He stalks the brown like a hunter stalks a trophy elk, and has researched their feeding habits, where they hold in the water, and their behavioral characteristics. Chris has even developed special tackle and refined flies for hunting browns.

In *Brown Trout Fly Fishing* Chris takes you with him to the streams and the lakes and shows you how to find and consistently catch brown trout. Unlike most books on fishing strategy that put you to sleep, Chris' book is as entertaining as it is informative. After spending many years guiding fishermen around the globe, and celebrities and former Presidents for his current boss Ted Turner, Chris has developed a pleasant streamside manner. You don't order a former President of the United States, you suggest to him that if he would try another fly, or cast upstream his fishing might improve. Chris writes the same way he guides, with suggestions, hints, and tips to make you a better fisherman.

In short, Chris Francis is not only a gentleman fly fisher, but as good a guide as you can find to introduce you to fishing for brown trout, a sport of the highest order. Keep this book handy, you'll find that you will be reading it often. *Brown Trout Fly Fishing* is the definitive book on brown trout fishing, and it will greatly improve your ability to catch more large brown trout.

Chuck Johnson
Gallatin Gateway, Montana
Winter 1996

CHAPTER ONE

HISTORY, NATURAL AND OTHERWISE

As I sit down to write this first chapter the urge to immediately start scribbling wildly about every single brown trout fly fishing technique, fly, piece of tackle, fishing partner or experience is almost overwhelming. My desire to present this information in a form that will hopefully prove of durable value is the only thing preventing me from making it one long enthusiastic sentence. Fly fishing for brown trout is sport of the highest order. Eventually it becomes all-consuming, finding no piece of information too arcane or any theory implausible.

This is a "how-to" book in the purest sense of the word. Attribute whatever prejudices you want. I'm very sure the sporting literature bullies will sputter and wheeze—this book will never, and was never intended to, be called great literature. In the end, if this book helps you catch more brown trout then it will have accomplished its original designs.

One more thing before you read any further, please promise yourself you will attempt to use good judgment and moderation, lest things get completely out of hand. As with any sport, if pursued to extremes, there will be innumerable pleasures punctuated by bouts of extreme anguish. Chasing brown trout with fly tackle is not exempt and will readily provide both. Happiness and absolute sorrow can both flow from a common wound. Using good judgment will keep these highs and lows in pleasant moderation.

Pleasures for me have included days spent on unspoiled waters, sight fishing to individual browns in clear water, knowing you just executed the perfect cast—before the fly ever touches the water, and of course the brief heart-stopping effect created by a brown trout peeling line off your reel. The anguish? Bankruptcy always looming on the horizon comes quickly to mind. As does long travel hours, failed

relationships, the seeming incapability of normal employment, and even being in a Russian helicopter wreck which registered a 9.7 on the Sphincter Scale. Yes, therapy has been considered. But if your first thoughts to all of this contain the words "worth it", I'd have to assume you have never caught a brown trout on a fly.

Anatomy Is Destiny

Definition of the brown trout should preclude any of the dissertations on habits, techniques or equipment. Predatory success requires an intimate

Brown about ready to be released. What separates them from other trout?

knowledge of the intended prey.

The earliest beginnings find brown trout being chased from the Arctic during the Eocene Epoch to the Glacial Epoch by, no surprise here, a glacier. The glacier eventually warmed, receded, and left native brown trout stranded in inland streams and lakes.

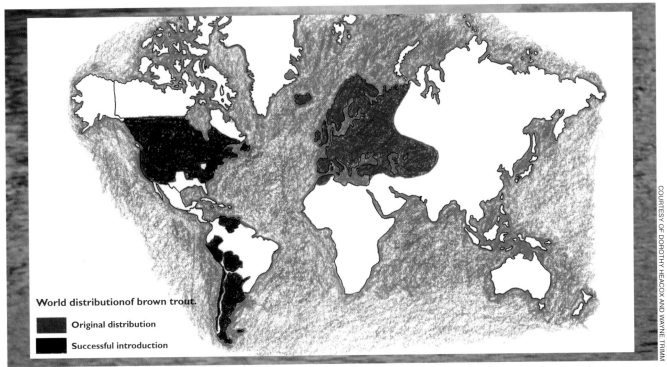

World distribution of brown trout.

■ Original distribution

■ Successful introduction

Brown trout that were capable migrated back to the sea eventually becoming sea trout. Those that stayed, brown trout. Sea trout are technically nothing more than brown trout which migrate from fresh to salt water. But, please bear in mind behaviorally there are vast differences requiring different angling techniques.

The brown trout left in inland waters found themselves located in Scotland, England, France, Germany, Austria; Russia, Asia, North Africa, Algeria and Morocco. Eventually, with help, the brown trout was carried and transplanted more often than any other fish species with the exception of the common carp. During these travels this wonderful sport fish eventually found its way to the United States.

How is the brown trout identified? The simplest and most logical starting place is probably the clinical definition of the professional fishery manager. Most biologists would probably agree with Dr. C.J.D. Brown. In his book *Fishes of Montana* he offers the following taxonomic solution:

1. Base of dorsal fin is shorter than head; dorsal rays fewer than 15.

2. Mouth is large with obvious teeth; more than 100 scales in lateral line.

3. Anal fin has 12 rays or less; brachiostegal rays (lines under head, below gill plate) are 12 or fewer.

4. Body and dorsal fin with small black or brown spots; prevomer (bone located on the roof of the mouth) flat with teeth along the entire length.

5. And finally...side of body with brown or blackish spots and usually red spots; caudal fin generally without spots, but may have few along margin. Yes, to the angler this is incredibly confusing but as we will see later, biologists enjoy small details.

People, fly fishermen in particular, have developed the overwhelming urge to turn and run at the least little mention of something that smacks

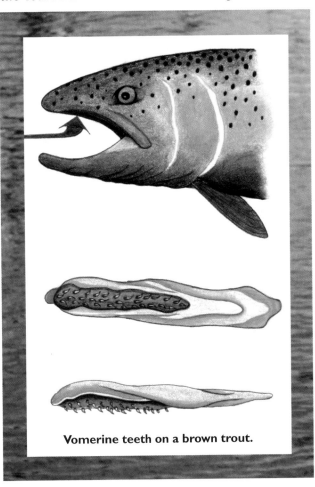

Vomerine teeth on a brown trout.

scientific. Please bear in mind the above chart has let you off easy because separate brown trout species could be "split" into a tremendous number of sub-species. While, for the truly demented, this can prove great fun during the long winter evenings it is of little interest to most anglers.

If the angler were to attempt to describe the same fish he would probably come up with a completely different description. Even with our current angling tendencies the brown trout remains one of the fly fisherman's most worthy quarries. If you are a dry fly advocate the apex of the experience is surely tricking a large selective brown into taking a delicately presented imitation. When it comes to dry fly fishing browns can be maddeningly difficult and serve to continually remind us we are not nearly as talented with a fly rod as we tend to tell other people.

Streamers are an entirely different matter. When the conditions are right large browns will take them with reckless abandon any time of the year. When a large brown is presented with one of these "big ugly" creations a certain raw predatory instinct takes over leaving nothing but carnage in the wake. Most anglers have heard the familiar story: "largest brown I ever saw came out of nowhere and grabbed the small fish I was in the process of reeling in..."

Brown trout also enjoy getting in the middle of a riffle during a strong emergence and feeding very selectively on nymphs. This makes them a strong favorite of the serious nymph fisherman, but a bane to the novice. Anglers new to nymph fishing would be well advised to look for rivers and streams with large populations of rainbows, brook trout or whitefish. Perfect your skills on these species before casting nymphs to browns. The best thing for the beginning nymph fisherman is to catch a lot of fish early on, which builds the all-important confidence so necessary to be a consistently successful nymph fisherman. Brown trout rarely provide these numbers. I have witnessed several talented anglers taking turns every five or six casts, switching nymph patterns, while sight fishing to a single brown so selective he never did take any of their offerings. All of these anglers were pretty advanced, but were still unable to hook up this particular fish.

In the end it seems the brown trout is almost custom designed for the fly rod. Contrary to some of the cracker-barrel experts browns really will jump after hooked and there are few fish that will fight as brilliantly. A fly angler's definition of the brown trout is probably best described in the words of one friend, "big fun."

Details, Details

Brown trout are fall spawners usually finding their mates and respective locations between October and December. They usually become sexually mature in the third year of life with females of 16 inches in length (or longer) producing between 1,200 and 1,600 eggs. Females will locate shallow, well-oxygenated riffles in which to spawn. Experience has shown me the preferred spawning gravel is almost always 3/4" in diameter. The female will deposit eggs onto the redd while the male simultaneously fertilizes them with milt. Eggs hatch 50 days later, usually leaving the redd in March or April. Browns have been known to occasionally hybridize with brook trout producing infertile offspring. These progeny are known as "tiger" trout and are rarely caught or located.

Growth and life expectancy varies considerably. Actual growth will not only vary region to region, but more accurately drainage to drainage. In Montana, where I live, brown trout habitat and growth can certainly be considered in the upper 10 percent; it produces brown trout growth as follows:

Year Of Life	Average Length
1	4 inches
2	8 inches
3	12 inches
4	14 inches
5	16 inches
6	18-20 inches

It might serve a brown trout angler well to remember this scale next time he is being told of where multiple browns over 20" are being caught. Oh, it happens occasionally, but as you can see the odds are really against it. Most brown trout will not live past four to five years of age. How long an individual brown will live depends on genetics and environmental factors. As a rule of thumb, brown trout populations at higher elevations, where the food supply is limited and the growing season shorter, will regularly have fish older than the six to seven year life expectancy.

Early in the brown trout's relocation it was thought it could "bear water several degrees warmer than *fontinalis* (brook trout) and therefore is adapted to a wider range." Turns out this astute observation was more than correct. Optimum temperature for stability, growth and survival is between 59° F and 66° F. Only if the temperature reaches above 81° F will browns readily begin to die.

Does the brown trout have any negative attributes? They are not native to North America. There I said it! It's out in the open! And yes while we are at it we better also mention, in some cases, it can outcompete native strains of fish. For this reason the brown trout has recently fallen out of vogue with the professional fishery manager. Before judgment is harshly passed allow a hasty comparative finger to be pointed toward the native brook trout which is now the most common trout of all. It is not surprising to find Western populations of brook trout in numbers greater than 5000 fish per mile—all of them five inches long, providing fine table fare but no real sport (I can hear the screams already). At the same time there are documented cases of brown trout coexisting in Arizona with the delicate native Apache trout. While both brookies and browns can be tough on natives and other species the brown trout's sporting qualities are far more desirable for the fly angler. The "non-native" issue has been a concern since the brown's earliest introductions. In some of the first writings Mr. Fred Mather, who, as you will see, was among the first people to bring the species into the United States, addresses this topic. In an 1887 *Bulletin of the United States Fish Commission*, Mather penned a piece entitled "Brown Trout in America." In part he wrote: "Some anglers have objected to the introduction of brown trout in our streams because they grow too fast and might eventually kill our native fish. To this I say: "Let 'em do it if they can and the 'fittest' will survive; but they can't do it." Mather goes on to explain native fish will always have the upper hand because they evolved in their home streams and the brown trout did not. Well...in some cases this worked, others were certainly less than stellar. Whether or not the decision was a good one or not becomes largely academic (philosophical). The whole mess seems to fizzle while trying to figure out what rights trout have, and if native trout have more rights than those that have been introduced. Once again, I suspect the serious brown trout angler finds this of little interest since the brown trout has already been introduced and by all indications is a survivor here to stay.

Ever since Norman Maclean's *magnum opus*, *A River*

Runs Through It, the person who could be loved but not helped seems to have become the standard fly fishing storyline. If the same storyline is applied to trout, the brown trout would surely surface as the protagonist. As of this writing brown trout have been finning around in American waters in excess of 115 years. While it is still early in the process, very few other fish populations have become so stable with so little effort. During this time very little, other than the initial transplants, has been done to increase their numbers and yet they have thrived. But, they are still not exactly welcomed with open arms by everyone. The tales surrounding the introduction of brown trout are rich and very lengthy. The Fred Mather story is certainly the commonly accepted history surrounding the subject, but there is a brief narrative which predicates it by four or five years.

The Gilbert Introduction

Fish culture (hatcheries), as we know it, was new to America but was already being ardently practiced in other parts of the world since the 1700s. Salmon eggs, probably Atlantic, were the first of the salmonids to be shipped. While they were not the first in fish culture, the British were the first to make it very common, and did more than anybody else to perfect the shipment of fertilized fish eggs. The brown trout is almost a British national identity, and they went to great lengths to ship them.

The March 29, 1881, *New York Times* has the article "A Fish Exhibition" on the front page. Judging from the location of the article this exhibition appears to have been pretty big news. The article, among other things, states: "There will be 40 English trout from W.S. Gilbert's Old Colony ponds, which are supposed to be hardier than American fish." This is one of the first mentions of, what must surely be, brown trout being in the United States. (It appears the newspaper made an error. In all of the other literature W.S. Gilbert is listed as W.L.) How in the world did Mr. Gilbert get his hands on brown trout eggs in 1881?

Here the story gets a little fuzzy, but it appears to center around a British father and son team by the last name of Ramsbottom. Thaddeus Norris wrote the first major work on fish culture in the United States. His 1868 book *American Fish-Culture* probably gives us our first look into the Ramsbottom personality, he writes: "Many persons in France and England, for amusement or the novelty of the thing, have miniature hatching apparatus in their houses." Robert Ramsbottom from Clitheroe, England was obviously this kind of person.

Ramsbottom, a fly fishing tackle manufacturer, whose 1854 book *The Salmon And Its Artificial Propagation* contained not only his tackle catalog in the back, but the last sentence: "Why not introduce the practice of Artificial Propagation into the colonies, into every suitable river of our vast empire, in both

hemispheres?" Trout for all—written like a true fly fisherman! What is unclear is how the Ramsbottom clan hooked up with Mr. Gilbert. Rumor has it the younger Ramsbottom had been brought (sent?) to America to run a hatchery. We are left to assume it was the Old Colony ponds under Gilbert's control. Shipping eggs across oceans, however, was nothing new to the Ramsbottoms. Norris also tells us: "the younger Ramsbottom was in Australia in 1864 waiting for a shipment of salmon eggs from his father." This proves they had plenty of experience prior to 1881.

It all fits very well. Once the younger Ramsbottom was in the United States with a hatchery, close to a major port, at his disposal, senior Ramsbottom just shipped one of the moist moss-lined boxes full of brown trout eggs to his son. There were supposedly 4,000 eggs shipped. Many of these did not endure the long journey and perished in transit. Of the 4,000 originally shipped Gilbert was only able to hatch 25. Since 25 were not enough for introduction into local waters they probably used them for Gilbert's exhibition. Brown trout would have to wait another three years before they would be introduced into "the colonies."

The Mather Introduction

An early pioneering fish culturist by the name of Mr. Fred Mather (who incidentally bears an uncanny resemblance to Colonel Sanders of fried chicken fame) is generally credited with bringing the brown trout to the United States from Germany in 1883. An article appeared on the fifth page of the February 24, 1883 issue of the New York Times entitled "The Werra's Quick Passage." It described the German steam-ship which had arrived a day earlier, in record time, carrying $260,000 in coins, 1,088 immigrants and some 80,000 brown trout eggs (it should probably be noted two strains of browns were mixed; 60,000 from a lake; the remainder from a small stream). The eggs were a personal present from Baron Friedrich von Behr, then president of the Deutscher Fischerei-Verein (German Fishery Society), to Fred Mather. The story of how Mr. Mather would be the one to receive these eggs falls just short of epic.

Fred Mather bought a farm near Honeoye Falls, New York and began raising trout for sale in 1868. He found the complex technology (at the time) necessary for the task rather appealed to him. The primary demand for trout during this era was for either stocking ponds at sporting clubs or more likely for sale as food to individuals or restaurants. Most of the latter were sold by a small group of fishmongers at New York's Fulton Market. Literature available during this time period suggests the fish business was fairly lucrative for the few who were already in operation. New competition, in sales or production, was not exactly embraced with open arms. Mather's newcomer status not only bothered him but stuck with him for some time.

Trout caught from the Madison River in 1919. If you look closely you can recognize the brown trout.

When he wrote his book entitled Modern Fish Culture some 32 years later the second paragraph states: "Fifteen miles west of me a man was breeding trout, but he did not approve of what he considered an invasion of his particular domain, and no information could be had in that quarter..." After some research it turns out the man Mather is describing is none other than Seth Green. Green had set up the first hatchery in the United States in 1864 on Caledonia Creek and his name still carries the title "Father of American Fish Culture." The rivalry between Mather and Green would escalate, turning long and intense, spanning both their careers and only stopping short of violence.

Two years after Mather had started his hatchery, and he had finally been accepted into the trade, he recognized a need to establish set prices for trout. In 1870, Mather with about 20 other varied trout culturists and fishmongers started the American Fish Culturist Association (now called the American Fisheries Society). If they initially formed this group for price gouging it was soon forgotten and they concerned themselves with a wide range of national fishery interests and political lobbying. Among other things the Association would eventually force the U.S. government to form the U.S. Fish Commission. Minutes from the early meetings reveal updates on everything from the sponge fisheries of Florida to the early musings on rainbow trout, if given the opportunity, possibly being migratory. The newly-formed Association also gave Mather and Green an organized forum for their on-going squabble. Within the framework of the American Fish Culturist Association and the U.S. Fish Commission they would fight about hatchery locations, fish classifications and eventually, credit for bringing the brown trout to the United States.

As with any organization with even the smallest amount of politics involved, the whole organization quickly divided into two camps, complete with fringe players who darted back and forth between the two as it suited their respective goals. The two camps consisted on one side of Green and his angling buddy and co-author, administrator Robert Barnwell Roosevelt. Mather was fortunate to have several administrators on his side. Prominent New York fishmonger Eugene G. Blackford, who would later help Mather get a Federal fishery for his imported brown trout eggs, but more importantly the first director of the U.S. Fish Commission, Professor Stephen F. Baird. As these groups and their constituents fell in and out of power of the American Fish Culturist Association, so did their pet projects. Oddly enough the only issue which all seemed to agree upon was transplanting any kind of new fish they could get their hands on, and the Mather camp had fallen behind. Fish sales at Fulton Market must have been very competitive, with the showcasing of a new species attributed with increased sales. The charismatic Green had already been the first to successfully transport and stock shad into California's Sacramento River, and among the first to bring rainbows from the West to the East Coast.

In 1874 Fred Mather finally received his chance to catch up. Baird appointed him as an assistant of the U. S. Fish Commission. One of Mather's first government assignments was to travel to Europe looking for new species and techniques. In 1880 the International Fisheries Exposition was to be held in Berlin. Bureaucracies, unlike businesses, usually send their best and brightest first, and the most charismatic second. This seems especially true with new technology. While Seth Green possessed the charm it was Fred Mather who was chosen as the American delegate to the Berlin Exposition.

It was here he met Baron von Behr who took him fishing for brown trout in the Black Forest. Being a keen fly fisherman, Mather was so impressed with the trout, talks of importation probably started immediately. True to his word, three years later, von Behr was to send Mather the first of several shipments, 80,000 brown trout eggs that were delivered on the steam-ship *Werra*.

Five days later the eggs were moved to a Federal hatchery at Cold Springs Harbor, where Mather, after

MR. PAT BARNES

Trout caught from the Lower Madison River around 1920.

another long battle with the Green camp, was now in charge. From Cold Springs Hatchery the eggs were ordered dispersed to more Federal hatcheries in Northville, Michigan and Caledonia, New York. Chief Superintendent at Caledonia was none other than Seth Green. Green was not going to let an opportunity to discredit his archenemy slip by. If you read between the lines of the early history of fish culture it hints where Green was headed.

Because of the poor condition of the eggs upon their arrival only a little more than half of the 80,000 eggs were still worth dispersing to the other hatcheries. Since Mather was in charge of dividing up the eggs he kept about 16,000 eggs and sent the equivalent amount to the Michigan hatchery. He only sent Green about 10,000 eggs. When it was time for the three hatchery superintendents to report their individual successes to the Commission the following year Mather had only been able to successfully raise 4,000 eggs. The superintendent from the Michigan hatchery reported a similar success rate. Green claimed, even though he was shorted on the egg distribution, he was able to raise over half of his allotment—providing more brown trout fry than the others! It is commonly believed this was in fact not true, and was done only to get at Mather. Whether it was true or not remains unknown, but Green's next move would not only infuriate Mather it would also have an effect which still surrounds brown trout today.

Since the arrival of the eggs, Mather had been calling the fish "brown trout." Green was able to get hold of the press and not only introduce the name "German trout", but also eluded to the fact that he was the one to first introduce them! While this barb incensed Mather, he had no way of realizing the full impact this term was going to have. The implications would extend well into the next century.

The fry from the first shipment of eggs were kept in holding ponds at all three hatcheries so they could not only be displayed but used as brood stock as well. Mather so enthusiastically showed these fish to everyone who would look he eventually managed to kill all but a few fish from all of the rough handling. The browns at Northville and Caledonia were reportedly doing well.

Another gift of 70,000 eggs was sent by von Behr the following year. This time the sister ship of the *Werra*, the *Donau*, carried the eggs and arrived in New York on February 5, 1884. Once again the eggs were split by Mather and dispatched to the same hatcheries, with the addition of some eggs going to the U.S. Fish Commission hatchery in Wytheville, Virginia.

The Stocking

Very few of the eggs sent to the Virginia hatchery survived. It was fry from the eggs of this second shipment sent to the Northville, Michigan hatchery that would be the first brown trout stocked into American waters. By now the U.S. Fish Commission was a little more organized so there is a detailed written record of this particular stocking. During this period transporting fish (or anything else for that matter) that were to be stocked were sent on the railroad. The rail car carrying the fish was stopped on a bridge spanning the desired watercourse, the side door opened, and the fish were deposited over the edge of the trestle.

The first stocking of brown trout into American waters would be carried out the same way. U.S. Fish Commission Car No. 2, loaded with 75,000 lake and 4,900 brown trout fry, left the Northville hatchery at 8 a.m. on April 11, 1884. Car No. 2 was then hooked to the Flint and Pere Marquette train which was headed to Baldwin, Michigan. Later the same day after the lake trout fry had been dumped, Car No. 2 rolled to a stop on a small railroad trestle over the Baldwin River. Here on this northern branch of the Pere Marquette River a can containing brown trout fry was unceremoniously emptied of its contents and the brown trout was finally delivered into American waters. Browns would be planted into both Iowa and

Maine streams later this same year. The next six years would see browns stocked in at least 15 other states. Brown trout were to spread like wildfire and would eventually help form the backbone of fly fishing in the United States.

The chart below was comprised by Cecil E. Heacox in 1972 for his book *The Complete Brown Trout*, which was published two years later. Some dates are approximate, and where no date appears no introduction has been attempted. The only changes I have made to the original chart is where research after 1972 has further refined the dates.

The Controversy

Several friends of mine are fisheries biologists with the Montana Department of Fish, Wildlife and Parks. They are all veterans of many public meetings, and jokingly refer to their instructions from taxpayers as: "Big fish; lots of 'em." This creed holds just as true now as it did at the turn of the century. Suddenly fish culturists outside of New York, who up until now had been treated with benign amusement, could make a management decision which would excite anglers.

Introduction Dates of Brown Trout

State, etc.	Year	State, etc.	Year
Alabama	1942 (unsuccessful)	North Carolina	1900
Alaska	—	North Dakota	1954
Arizona	1924	Ohio	1885
Arkansas	1949	Oklahoma	—
California	1894	Oregon	1897
Colorado	1903	Pennsylvania	1886
Connecticut	1893	Rhode Island	1940
Delaware	1968	South Carolina	1900
Florida	—	South Dakota	1891
Georgia	1900	Tennessee	1900
Hawaii	1935 (unsuccessful)	Texas	—
Idaho	1918	Utah	1895
Illinois	1900	Vermont	1892
Indiana	1900	Virginia	1960
Iowa	1884	Washington	1933
Kansas	—	West Virginia	1930
Kentucky	—	Wisconsin	1887
Louisiana	—	Wyoming	1890
Maine	1884	Puerto Rico	1938
Maryland	1929	Alberta	1924
Massachusetts	1887	British Columbia	1933
Michigan	1884	Manitoba	1943
Minnesota	1888	New Brunswick	1921
Mississippi	—	Newfoundland	1886
Missouri	1966	Nova Scotia	1925
Montana	1889	Ontario	1913
Nebraska	1889	Prince Edward Island	—
Nevada	1930	Quebec	1890
New Hampshire	1887	Saskatchewan	1924
New Jersey	1912	Northwest Territories	—
New Mexico	1926	Yukon	—
New York	1883		

MR. JEROME GROFF

This is the bridge in Baldwin, Michigan where brown trout were introduced into the United States.

Brown trout had proven adaptable and durable with an almost "can't-miss" reputation for producing large trout in varied regional waters. Brown trout were stocked with reckless abandon and anglers were extremely supportive in anticipation of trying their hand at catching this new import.

Unfortunately no love affair lasts this long without a crisis or two. Oddly enough it was Thaddeus Norris's first book, published in 1864, *American Angler's Book* which, in a roundabout way, would eventually lead to public outcry over the releasing of brown trout into American waters. The *American Angler's Book* contained one of the first descriptions of fishing with a dry fly. This feat went largely unnoticed by the angling masses. Exceptions to this were gentlemen by the last names of LaBranche, Keene and Rhead. While these men would bring the dry fly to America it would require one more to make it a popular fly and technique.

The other person who did not fail to notice the dry fly passage was a famous angler by the name of Theodore Gordon. He not only noticed, but was to get very serious about fishing dry flies in the upcoming years. In fact Gordon may not only have been the first major promoter of American dry fly fishing, but quite possibly could have been the first certified trout bum in the nation. His beautifully hand-tied dries (tied in order to eat and continue to fish) would popularize an obscure modern fly angling method which would forever change the sport. Dry fly patterns and techniques had already spread quickly, becoming the preferred method for taking trout. This is where the problems for brown trout would begin.

Theodore Gordon was a first rate angler and very

few other fly fishermen of the time possessed either his skill or commitment. The end result would be a large majority of dry fly anglers who were able to catch several creels full of native brook trout but almost no brown trout.

Theodore Gordon started writing for *Forest and Stream* around 1900, but in all these articles (letters actually) he never said dry fly fishing was the best way to catch fish. These unsuccessful anglers started to realize a noticeable decline in the brook trout fishing where brown trout had been introduced. While the jury was still out, brown trout began to be viewed with suspicion. As for Mr. Gordon he would continue to catch all the species of trout available to him in upstate New York with dry flies until his death, after the start of World War I.

World War I was no different from any other war we have been involved in, in the sense that its start was quickly followed by a fierce patriotism spreading across the homefront. Everything German was bad. No exceptions. German browns, a name Seth Green coined almost 30 years before, would not prove to be an exception. Anglers cried: "They are trash fish, and won't take a fly." Studies labeled the brown a "poor angling investment." Suspicion had turned to contempt. These feelings would persist until the end of the war, without one word about angler ability being mentioned.

But brown trout were here to stay and eventually technique and ability would catch up with the keen senses of these imports. Brown trout are now taken regularly with a myriad of patterns and are now the only fish most hard-core dry fly fishermen consider challenging enough.

CHAPTER TWO

RIVERS AND STREAMS

Rivers

As mentioned earlier fly fishermen have videos, magazines, seminars, expert advisors, fishing partners and equipment machined to .001 of an inch. Brown trout only have their own visceral abilities/reactions and the watery depths. Yet, consistently catching a river-dwelling brown trout remains one of the sport's most difficult challenges, surrounded with unanswered questions. You will never answer all of them, but many answers can be found in the depths of a river. When writing about brown trout and where to find them in a river it is tempting to describe a few streambed features (easily identified, of course) known to attract browns, toss in a few popular rivers for examples and be done with it. Unfortunately this would do the serious brown trout angler a great disservice. Brown trout rivers vary enormously, with the more productive ones in a constant state of change. Heraclitus, the great philosopher,

Changes in velocity will help you recognize good areas to look for browns. The author about ready to release a good fish.

once said, "you can never step in the same river twice." Good advice. Once we couple all the dynamics with brown trout behavior, it becomes amazing we ever catch any of the brutes at all.

The most important thing to learn about finding brown trout in rivers is their location tendencies. These tendencies can be isolated using a very simple equation:

$$\text{River Behavior} + \text{Brown Trout Behavior} = \text{Brown Trout Location Tendencies}$$

Identifying and understanding this equation's two parts is the best way to begin. River behavior is a vast and interesting subject, but the one aspect we want to focus on is water velocity. Water velocity determines where brown trout feed, rest and spawn. Once you learn to recognize velocity changes, especially as they relate to food production, these places will stick out like a giant neon "Fish Here" sign. River velocity increases as the width of a river decreases. The most common place this occurs is in riffles. Riffles are the Midwest of any river, producing food at higher rates than any other part of the system. Several things happen all at once to allow this. Because of the increased velocity these shallow areas are usually void of any silt or sand and can be identified by their gravel and cobble deposits.

Of all the substrate found in a river, cobble-sized (roughly ten and one quarter inches in diameter, if you must know) rocks are the most productive. If you have never thought of river rocks as being productive now might be the time to start. This is something to ponder next time you see a pile of them on the river bank next to an irrigation project. These medium sized rocks are what stoneflies, mayflies and caddisflies demand. They not only provide a large surface for adherence but also a convenient break from the faster water which they need for respiration and food consumption. None of this process is hurt by the fact riffles are shallow, allowing sunlight to penetrate the entire water depth causing photosynthesis, which creates food for the insects. Unfortunately, this same sunlight also makes browns feel vulnerable and skittish. Riffles on rivers with even the slightest bit of angling pressure are usually best fished in times of low light or heavy drift before an emergence.

Another problem with riffles is that brown trout are unable to turn these rocks over and feed on these insects like a coastal brown bear on salmon. Nor are brown trout built to feed in the heavy current like rainbows. Once again, water velocity comes to the rescue promoting an insect marvel called drift. Drift is the downstream movement of aquatic insects. Many studies have been completed to figure out if this is a passive or voluntary journey. It is not unlike the Arctic lemmings who, at regular intervals, throw themselves off high cliffs into the ocean rather than face overpopulation. To a point, river velocities create more drift and subsequently more food for trout.

Since brown trout are not as well adapted as rainbows to feeding in heavy current they must pay closer attention to energetic profitability. Don't panic. While this sounds complicated it simply means a brown trout (or to some extent, any living being) must consume more calories than it expends. A riffle, while it produces the most food also has the heaviest flows. Brown trout want to be as close as possible to riffles without expending the required energy needed to stay there. This forces them to seek out low-velocity pockets to accomplish their goals.

Successful brown trout fishing will constantly challenge you to locate these pockets. The obvious seams and breaks in the current are created by rocks, logs, converging current speeds, river banks and if you fish in Montana the occasional discarded '57 Buick body.

Where to fish a low-velocity pocket created by a rock, will depend on the size of the rock. If the rock is four or five feet in diameter or smaller, concentrate your efforts along the sides and in the back eddy behind the rock. If you are fishing from a moving drift boat and only have time for one cast, focus on the eddy directly behind the rock.

Some angling writers have written about how trout will hold "backwards" behind rocks, facing into the micro-current created by the back eddy. Observation and experience have shown this idea to be in error. While the back eddies behind rocks definitely force an upstream current, this current does not carry enough food for the fish to hold facing into it. If any forage fish swam by (headed downstream) the brown trout would initially have to fight the current (upstream micro-current) in pursuit. Trout hold facing upstream in the seam of a back eddy. On one side is the river headed downstream and the other side is the upstream micro-current. This enables the fish to move up and down the river by effortlessly moving a few inches to either side. Eagles and other large birds ride thermals in much the same manner. This way insect-drift in the main river current can be watched with little effort. If a forage fish passes by, the brown trout simply turns sideways into

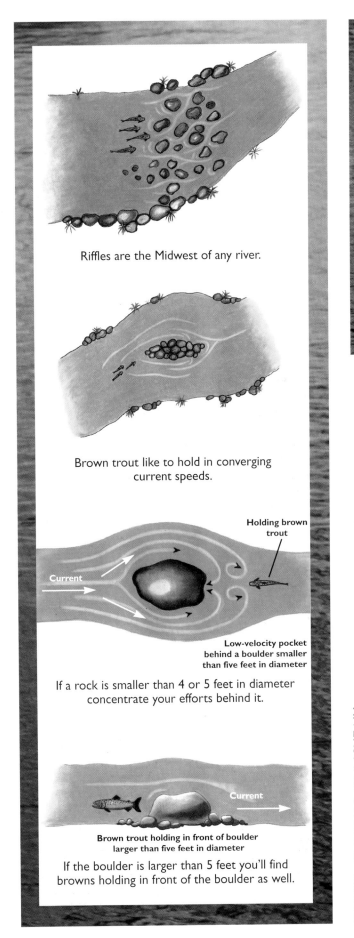

Riffles are the Midwest of any river.

Brown trout like to hold in converging current speeds.

Holding brown trout

Current

Low-velocity pocket behind a boulder smaller than five feet in diameter

If a rock is smaller than 4 or 5 feet in diameter concentrate your efforts behind it.

Current

Brown trout holding in front of boulder larger than five feet in diameter

If the boulder is larger than 5 feet you'll find browns holding in front of the boulder as well.

Large pools can sometimes yield large browns.

the current and the current actually aids in downstream movement.

Rocks larger than five feet in diameter will require you pass a fly in front of them as well. The larger surface area of these rocks creates a vortex (Thorassic, I think) on the upstream edge providing a low-velocity holding area.

Logs and fallen trees provide excellent holding cover for brown trout. Let's say you happen to be in the front of a drift boat floating down the Yellowstone River casting a large weighted streamer. On your next cast, you have a choice of stripping your streamer under a log resting on the water's surface or one which is completely submerged. Which would you choose? Hopefully your choice was the latter. Brown trout, especially in fall and winter, prefer to hold under completely submerged cover rather than cover partially above-water. This extra depth enhances their vision and makes drifting food sources more available.

Undercut river banks are the quintessential submerged brown trout cover. Although fishing them can be a little tricky, (we'll cover this in the streamer chapter) undercut banks will hold a tremendous number of browns. The more vegetation that is present not only makes fish sturdier, but it is also more capable of delivering both terrestrial and aquatic insects. Undercut banks are the first thing lost when the U.S. Army Corps of Engineers, or anybody else, shows up to save a cattle-trampled river bank by "putting down a little rip-rap." All of these low-velocity pockets are pretty easy to identify and locate, and will serve the brown trout angler well. Low-velocity areas that hold even more fish are tougher to identify and find.

As the river channel widens this causes a decrease in velocity, creating pools and tail-outs. Here the river surface smooths out due to lack of water friction. Loss of velocity causes the river to lose its ability to carry the fine silt and sediment it successfully blasted through the previous riffle. Drifting aquatic insects also settle out of the current at this time. Day in and day out this is where a brown will consume the majority of its food. Many fly fishermen are overwhelmed with the prospect of adequately covering large pools. This is unwarranted. A simple principle in hydrology can prevent many useless hours when

fishing pools. The first thing to remember when fishing pools is a river's maximum velocity occurs at the surface in the center of the streambed. This principle is routinely ignored. The following example is not intended to be self-glorifying, but rather to illustrate the importance of this often overlooked principle.

Nymph fishing for brown trout on the upper Madison River is one of the great joys in life. Judging from the increased number of other fly fishers there are many who would concur. It was the weekend and the river was very crowded, with almost every pool requiring a wait. After I rowed the boat into a pocket to pass time before my turn, I had the opportunity to watch two fly fishermen fish through the pool. They both had excellent equipment and were more than proficient with their casting. Strike indicators on both their leaders implied they were nymph fishing. Both fished the entire pool without even a strike. There were several reasons for this. They had waded as far out from the bank as their waders would allow, and thus were standing in the prime holding lie on the edge of the pool without fishing this area first. This put their casts right through the middle of the pool. Although premature, this was OK, as it was also good holding water. But, I could see the second problem from watching their flies enter the water. They were using unweighted nymphs with no weight

**Browns like to feed on nymphs
flushed out of the riffles.**

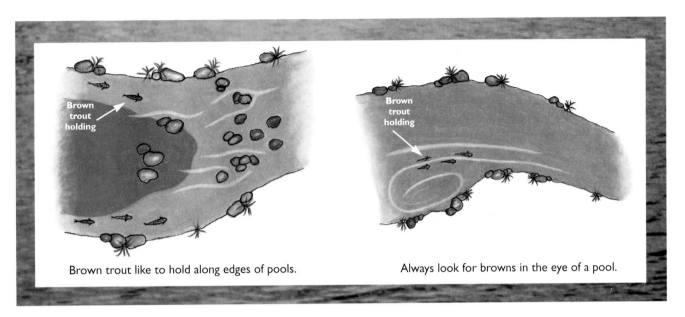

Brown trout like to hold along edges of pools.   Always look for browns in the eye of a pool.

on their leaders. As a result, the water surface in the center of the river, which is hardest for a trout to hold in, was being fished. This is a pity because these two fellows had probably spent a considerable amount of personal resources to make this trip happen and elementary knowledge was preventing them from catching fish.

Brown trout hold on the bottom and sides of pools. Sides of pools should always be fished first, before wading through them to fish the bottom of the pool. This is especially important in areas with light angling pressure. Sides of pools in these areas will hold more browns than in places that are crowded. Experience has shown once a brown is continually spooked it will be nightfall before he quits sulking on the pool bottom and returns to the edge. Pool bottoms are the preferred feeding areas. Brown trout holding in them are more likely to be larger, stronger and more dominant. Brown trout ideally like pools six to seven feet deep.

The eye of a pool is another excellent place to find feeding brown trout. Pools will always have at least one eye and sometimes two. If a pool has only one eye, chances are it will be located on the inside of a bend in the river immediately where the riffle ends. A pool with two eyes happens when a riffle terminates into a pool on a straightaway. Pools and their eyes are both good places to fish during midday. Their relative depth give brown trout a feeling of security. If any overhead cover is present, all the better, it will make the eye a constant producer. I can think of several scattered around southwestern Montana which have produced many browns for me over the years. Currents in eyes of pools are really nothing more than giant back-eddies, similar to those found behind rocks. Unlike low-velocity pocket water created behind midstream rocks, the eye of a pool, will have enough reverse current to cause browns to hold faced into the micro-current. Eyes large enough to cause this are generally large single ones located on the inside of large sweeping turns in the river. When fishing a pool's eye always work the down-

stream (main current) tail first. This will prevent you from "lining" fish. Be sure to position yourself far enough back to avoid being spotted by any fish facing downstream. If you are very lucky and look very hard you might locate an eye with a low-velocity lens directly upstream.

Low-velocity lenses are the most difficult of all fluvial features to locate and, as you have probably already guessed, consistently hold the greatest number of brown trout. Low-velocity lenses are extremely difficult to isolate, but usually can be found just upstream from the eye of a pool. I'll tell you right now there are far more eyes without them than there are with them. Look hard. Observable indicators are usually large obstructions, on the inside of tight bends in the river, which cause a subtle back-watering to occur in a section of the riffle just upstream from the obstruction. This will cause a low-velocity lens with the same surface water speed as the rest of the riffle, but with an underwater current break near the streambed. What happens is the large obstruction acts like a dam and backs more water up over one particular section of the riffle, while not backing up enough to cause a noticeable change in current speed. As a result, if you look very closely, this will almost always result in a small cross current within the riffle as this water is forced to slide to the outside of the turn, around the obstruction. What this means for brown trout is an area, actually in the food-producing riffle, that is energetically profitable. Water chop on the surface provides enough overhead cover to make browns feel secure any time of the day. At midday it is possible to find browns gorging themselves on nymphs drifting through the riffle. This creates a brown trout fly fisherman's nirvana. By using the correct nymph it is not uncommon to pull six or seven browns, on nine or ten casts, out of one of these areas.

Occasionally low-velocity lenses will be created by streambed features alone and there won't be any observable obstruction back-watering part of the riffle. When you think this might be the case go ahead and look for the cross current, but then check if it is possible to view this section of river from a higher observation point while the sun is at your back. Low-velocity lenses will appear as dark blue "discs" while the rest of the riffle remains a bluish-green. Quite a few rivers have high, steep banks that can be a great help. Getting the proper sunlight can be the more difficult problem. Depending on the riffle's location you may not have suitable sunlight until sunset. If the riffle is halfway on a six hour float, you might have to get a little creative to get a look.

Like almost everything else worthwhile, low-velocity lenses are not without their nuisances and frustrations. The largest nuisance is, once again, velocity. These areas are so subtle, changes in flow rate can quickly change their complexion, especially on tailwater fisheries where flow rates are changed regularly. Low-water lenses that hold many brown trout on one visit, may not be capable of holding any under a different flow regime. The biggest frustration is when you locate a riffle with all the telltale signs, but you can never find fish holding in the low-water lens. I know of several of these and they are maddening. The best advice I can give you is to keep trying them every time you are fishing the stretch of water where they are located. Eventually you will come across them when the conditions are right and they are holding fish. When this occurs be sure to make a mental note of the river's velocity. Very few fly fishermen pay close enough attention when they are on the water to locate one of these lenses. Look hard next time you are on your favorite brown trout river. When you find one, you will probably be the only person to fish it, even if there has been a crowd of anglers all day on the river ahead of you.

You should be aware some of the advice you have just read regarding brown trout holding water is really tailored to rivers which receive angling pressure. With the growth fly fishing has experienced in the last 10 years I know of fewer and fewer places which are not crowded. It is an observed fact disturbed brown trout act entirely different than those left unmolested. I only mention this for several reasons. First, a successful brown trout angler needs to be able to catch fish from rivers where other anglers fish. Secondly, and happily so, there are still a few places left where a resourceful angler can dodge the crowds and cast over undisturbed browns. Brown trout behavior varies radically between these two situations.

The first person to come to this realization was a Ph.D. candidate named Robert Bachman. Bachman, a former Naval submarine officer, was studying brown trout behavior at Pennsylvania State University. While his particular study had quite a bit to do with examining some of the constant mistakes made in fisheries' investigating techniques, it also was a landmark study which taught us a tremendous amount about brown trout behavior.

From 1976 to 1980 Robert Bachman spent April through September, every year, sitting in a camouflaged observation tower overlooking Spring Creek, a limestone stream in south-central Pennsylvania. The simple fact

Fred Kratz fishes some low-velocity lenses on the San Juan River in New Mexico.

Bachman was sitting in an observation tower and was not in the water represented the first time a fisheries researcher had been entirely removed from the brown trout behavior equation. What he observed was not only amazing, but revolutionary as well.

Bachman laid to rest many accepted "facts" all brown trout anglers held as gospel for a long time. "Facts" like brown trout always like to hide under overhanging banks, refuse to eat during the day and never feed in the middle of a riffle. Bachman found overhead cover has almost nothing to do with where brown trout choose to position—it almost all has to do with the fish choosing a proper feeding station. As a matter of fact 93 percent of all brown trout involved in the study fed at locations where overhead cover was entirely absent. Other statistics were also very interesting. Feeding, or a "sit-and-wait" behavior in a known feeding area, comprised more than 86 percent of all activity during daylight hours. An additional 8 percent of their time was spent returning to these areas after the brown trout had left them to pursue and capture other food items.

Other aspects of the study revealed some behavioral characteristics which fit very well with conventional brown trout wisdom. Larger browns tended to dominate the feeding lanes, but it was the larger browns which fed less often, and more selectively, than smaller ones. As brown trout grow in size, it becomes important they eliminate the smaller, less energetically profitable, food items from their diet. This behavior also leaves ample forage for the smaller browns in any given population. One other observation I found interesting was the fact that disturbed browns returned to their normal feeding patterns and places about 20 minutes after being disturbed. My personal experience mirrors Mr. Bachman's findings—like everyone else I was not smart enough to recognize it until he pointed it out.

Please remember this study was completed on a private section of creek, with no angling pressure. The way brown trout behave on crowded rivers is probably not their first choice. What this means to the brown trout angler is he must be very cognizant of the type of setting being fished. Browns inhabiting even the most crowded rivers can act like those in Spruce Creek, if you happen to be the first person to them during the day. Or, if you are fortunate enough to be able to consistently fish private water this might be the only way you ever see browns behave.

The take-home lesson from all of this is twofold. Never assume accepted brown trout "facts" are always as they are presented, and be very mindful of your approach—the fish you are looking for could be in the middle of the stream. In all but the most crowded situations you can never be sure if you are the first angler to fish a riffle for the day or not.

Always pay close attention to the position of sun. How you use this to your advantage will vary. The more years I fish for brown trout, the more this has changed. I used to be of the opinion you always wanted the sun in your face to prevent casting a shadow across the water. Now I feel this depends on how close to the feeding brown you wish to get. If your plan is to make your presentation from 15 yards away or more, having the sun in your face is probably a good idea. If you are going to attempt to get closer than this I now like to have the sun directly behind me. This not only puts the sun in the fish's eyes, it illuminates the trout, helping with a more accurate presentation. So long as you are careful of shadow direction, this will enable you to stand almost as close as you want. On many occasions browns can be caught from so close a proximity even the leader is almost too much line. For close work keep the sun at your back, and your shadow off to the side.

Streams

Streams are the life-blood of any river system. To the brown trout they help spawning, survival and growth. An excellent example of their importance to growth can be found in comparing two great Montana brown trout fisheries.

The Bighorn River is a tailwater fishery in southcentral Montana. It scarcely needs anything else in the way of an introduction unless you have been fly fishing in a box

Dr. J.M. Conley displays a nice brown. This brown fell for a small nymph.

for the last ten years. Yes, it is almost unbearably crowded during the summer, but (and this is a big but) it remains one of the most fertile brown trout fisheries in the world. The trout per mile figure is astounding. You catch many brown trout in the fifteen to eighteen inch range, and you can usually do it on dry flies twelve months of the year. The only thing missing is very large (in excess of 26", for the sake of argument) browns in any appreciable numbers. OK, every year you hear of several caught by some guy spin fishing in the after-bay with salad shrimp, but even this doesn't happen with any great regularity.

The Yellowstone River, on the other hand, is an entirely different matter. While it does not contain the trout per mile the Bighorn does, it accounts for many large browns every year. The Yellowstone is also very crowded during the summer. So what's the difference? Why does the Yellowstone have more large brown trout than the Bighorn? The Yellowstone does not have any dams on it preventing brown trout from reaching its tributaries. The stretch of the Bighorn everybody gets all excited about is sandwiched between Yellowtail Dam (the construction of which created this wonderful fishery) on one end and a large irrigation diversion dam on the other. There is a direct correlation between large brown trout and their having access to a river's tributaries. One sensible explanation is the larger size required for longer spawning migrations through increasing altitude. It simply requires a larger brown trout to reach these upper spawning areas.

Spawning season is when brown trout really move into the tributaries. Autumn spawning migrations account for over 93 percent of a brown trout's movement every year.

After arriving in these areas browns start to look for a place with acceptable water velocity in which to spawn. These places must have the needed flows to maximize egg production as well as substrate small enough to be moved by the fish when creating a redd. This brings up an interesting question about spawning brown trout.

Should we fish for them? This is a brown's most vulnerable time. For a short time every fall they become concentrated, and, with the right fly, very easy to catch. I'll tell you right now I've done it. In my youth this was the standard way to regularly catch large brown trout but, admittedly, a little something always seemed to be missing. It is not the fishing of browns on their spawning runs I am talking about. This is one of the finest times to fish for them. They fight wonderfully and are usually eager to take a fly.

What is being questioned is fishing for them when they are visibly on their redds. When this happens it is seldom the adults being caught that are in jeopardy. When a fly fisherman finds spawning browns he usually spooks fish off the redds that were closest to the bank he approached on. This done, he proceeds to wade across them to present a fly to the brown trout still on redds by the far side of the creek. There have been studies completed to quantify the effects wading has on fertilized eggs while they are in the redds. One wading across a redd, prior to the egg's hatching, killed 43 percent of the eggs present in that redd. Several daily wadings over the redd, throughout the ripening process killed all of the eggs. The other argument is, it is currently thought brown trout lay their eggs at night. This provides enough time for silt and sediment to sufficiently cover and cushion the eggs to protect them during wading. In either event female brown trout deposit most of their eggs in the rear of the oval shaped redd at about two and a half inches deep.

Even though it is legal to do so in most states, should you wade across redds while you fish? This is up to you. Remember this is a fishing book, not one on personal streamside conduct. A simple guideline might be how crowded the stream is. If you are the only one who knows about this area, the damage might only be 43 percent. If it is a stream or spring creek with tremendous pressure the loss could be far greater. In the end there is no such thing as the redd police, and the choice is yours.

Streams also provide brown trout a safeguard against threatening temperature ranges in a river. If a river's water temperature rises to levels a brown trout finds unacceptable then it will look for alternative habitat in streams. This will generally occur when the water temperature exceeds 67 degrees Fahrenheit. Brown trout will also stop feeding at this temperature.

Fall spawning areas also provide clues on where to fish when this happens. If brown trout are using a spawning area you can almost bet the area's streambed will also have some ground water seepage which helps provide oxygen for the eggs. Remember this for the dog-days of summer. Above that particular riffle will be a pool, or hole,

with a constant supply of cold spring water being delivered by the riffle.

Other good places to look for brown trout in streams are irrigation returns and bridges. Providing there is adequate water beneath a return, browns will hold nearby, or sometimes even directly underneath, waiting for forage fish to re-enter the stream. Bridges over streams are usually low enough to provide overhead cover. Unfortunately this only leaves the fly fisherman with a straight downstream presentation, but it is still worthwhile.

Brown Trout Movement

What causes brown trout to move (not counting migration, of course) in any body of water remains one of the great mysteries of the sport. One of the few sure things is that most movement in rivers occurs at night. Home ranges of younger (one year olds) brown trout will be about

66 feet, and if they move it will usually be upstream. Juveniles seek out slow riffle areas with large cobbles for protection. Older browns will range about two miles maximum during summer and winter. Spring and fall will find them travelling upwards of 12 miles. Once the older fish are in one of these seasonal areas they switch holding spots every two or three days. When switching holding areas older browns seldom go farther than a quarter of a mile.

If you ever get beaten by a large brown trout and would like a rematch these figures are good knowledge to have. A good example of this happened on the Bighorn River. Dr. J.M. Conley was fishing the Pale Morning Dun hatch and was skilled enough to hook, land and release a very nice 23-inch brown that was slurping the little mayflies from under the safety of an algae mat. While a 23-inch brown is one anyone will remember, this one had a very distinctive heron-caused scar on its left side. Dr. Conley

hooked this fish twice more during the week in the same general location.

As you read through the previous pages I'm sure you could think of several exceptions you have personally witnessed, and dozens more you have heard about, to every absolute given. Truth is, any game fish, much less one as crafty as a brown trout, is capable of quickly turning our best angling theories into nonsense. I mention this not to discourage or negate, but rather to hearten and support the serious brown trout fly fisherman. Please bear in mind the reason we remember these exceptions is because they are just that. Remembering and acknowledging exceptions will make you a better angler, but don't make the mistake of planning a day on the river around them. A good day of brown trout fishing should be planned around your ability to read water, and normal tendencies in brown trout behavior.

The Deschutes River near the lower bridge.

RIVERS AND STREAMS

CHAPTER THREE

LAKES AND PONDS

Zones and Layers

Lakes and ponds as they effect brown trout are a case study in bittersweet relationships. Browns in lakes will generally grow to a much larger size in a shorter period of time than they will in streams. However, they do become very difficult to catch not only with fly tackle but any other tackle (yes, even trolling gear), as well. This display of reluctance caused British angling scribe Geoffrey Bucknall to write: "Brown trout in our richer lakes tend to be dour bottom feeders, unpopular with those addicted to the surface rise." When was the last time you saw an advertisement in the back of a fly fishing magazine that stated: "Come let us guide you on our private ponds for large trophy brown trout." You see the same ads for rainbows all the time. One reason is browns in lake systems are more efficient and feed for much shorter periods of time than rainbows. But, don't pack it in quite yet.

The good news is I said they were difficult to catch—not impossible! If you pay close attention to detail and learn individual lakes well enough you will be able to consistently catch browns. Please bear in mind this isn't going to be the type of angling you are going to start to feel heady about after a week-long effort during your holiday. Brown trout lake fishing knowledge is hard won. Much more time is required to catch browns from a lake than a stream.

The largest difference between rivers and lakes is you no longer have the energetically-profitable holding areas to help you locate the fish. Wind and wave action will occasionally move food from areas of production but it will never equal the transportation of a river. As a matter of fact the whole energetic profitability theory becomes inverse. It is now counter-productive for the brown trout to stay located in one spot. If it wants to survive it must actively search out calories.

Natural lakes with brown trout populations will be the most consistent producers. Because natural lakes have been in existence the longest they tend to have a greater diversity of species which affords them a greater amount of stability. Unfortunately this natural lake and brown trout combination can be very difficult to find. Most of the natural lakes where I live, in the Rockies, are too high in altitude to provide the higher temperature range brown trout need to thrive.

For these reasons, reservoirs and drainage lakes, while second best, will be the kind of stillwater you'll want to focus your efforts on, especially in the West. The first question you need to answer is what role, if any, do artificial water fluctuations have on the system. While reservoir construction boomed in this country in the 1920s and 1930s it was not without reasons. Flood control, irrigation and power generation usually take water priority over fish in reservoirs. Drawdown has effects on oxygen levels, aquatic vegetation, invertebrates and a whole host of other variables. These periods of low water can have both negative and positive effects on a lake and its brown trout population. The different situations are almost infinite, so you'll have to keep a sharp eye for drawdown and the effects it has on your particular reservoir.

Brown trout anglers new to lake fishing often focus their efforts on smaller impoundments because the larger reservoirs tend to be intimidating. Very seldom is this good strategy. The total weight of any given population will be related to the size of the water body it resides in. Proportionally your chances are the same regardless of the size of the lake. In order to consistently find brown trout you must figure out where and how (and how often) you can consistently locate part, or all, of this population.

One of the first things we must look at to help us locate fish is something called thermal stratification. Thermal stratification comes in two types, seasonal and regular.

Seasonal thermal stratification occurs when an upper portion of a lake reaches 39 degrees Fahrenheit. At this temperature water attains maximum density. This block of "heavy water" will displace "lighter water" wherever it travels in the lake bed until it is cooled or warmed. Until this happens a giant mixing effect tends to put the fish off the bite. In brown trout lakes this process generally takes place in May or June with a chance of recurrence in the fall. Fishing during these periods is usually very poor, unless you can find a part of the lake not being effected.

As a little side note, this phenomenon can also be very important if you enjoy fishing tail-water streams. I can still remember an ill-fated trip to New Mexico's San Juan River. We had checked and thought of everything. By the time a fishing companion and I had driven south from Montana (OK, so we stopped at a few selected hot spots along the way and this portion of the trip took a little longer than expected) the reservoir had began to turnover. Everything was muddy. Be sure to find out what time of year turnover occurs before planning any long-range trips. The good thing seasonal thermal stratification does however is set the stage for a regular thermal stratification. Think of all three of these layers as nothing more than a horizontal temperature description of a lake.

The epilimnion is the warmest, upper most layer in any lake. It usually ranges anywhere from twenty to thirty feet in depth and will have a constant water temperature from top to bottom. The larger the body of water, the bigger the epilimnion will be. Light penetration in this zone is complete and photosynthesis occurs throughout. Most all of the lake's biological production and dissolved oxygen occurs in this layer.

Below the epilimnion is a thinner layer called the thermocline. This layer is a cool transitional zone associated with drastic temperature changes from top to bottom. While the thermocline is oxygenated it does not support the dissolved oxygen the warmer epilimnion does.

At the bottom is the hypolimnion. Not much happens here. Dissolved oxygen is close to, if not totally, nonexistent. Because of the size and makeup of the hypolimnion very little circulation occurs. It should be noted in smaller, shallower lakes and ponds this layer may not exist and you will find the thermocline extended all the way to the bottom.

Thermal stratification layers help locate browns, but in conjunction with their vertical counterparts the two can provide almost pinpoint accuracy.

Lake zones are the vertical counterparts of the thermal stratification layers. Lake zones also have three components. Remember thermal stratification layers are the horizontal temperature description of the lake, which leaves vertical production description for lake zones.

The shallow area around the perimeter of any given lake, where light can penetrate all the way to the bottom, is called the littoral zone. Almost all of a lake's forage production occurs in this area. Different aquatic plants found in the littoral zone tend to share the fact they are either

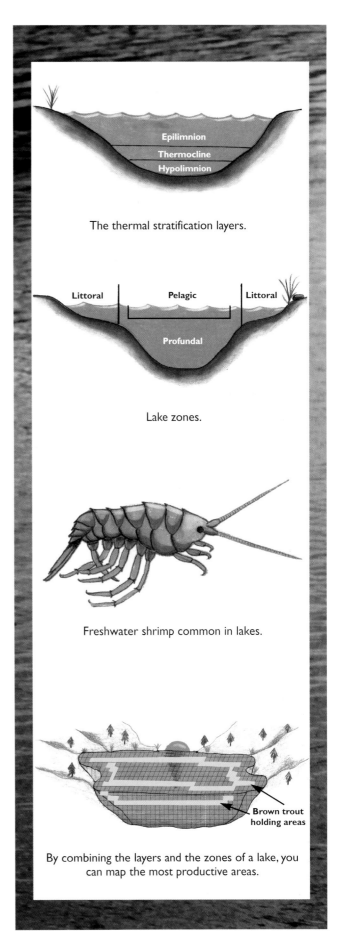

The thermal stratification layers.

Lake zones.

Freshwater shrimp common in lakes.

By combining the layers and the zones of a lake, you can map the most productive areas.

rooted in, or the plants' growth begins upward from, the lake bed. Certain types of algae, submersed rooted aquatic plants, emergent rooted aquatic plants and the occasional woody plants and trees cover all the types found in this zone. How does this information help the fly fisherman looking for brown trout in a lake? These plants are responsible for the primary production of energy (via photosynthesis) for the entire lake. All other living organisms in the lake are dependant on these primary producers for existence. In most lakes containing brown trout, dissolved oxygen is pretty high in this zone during the day with a small subtle decrease at night.

If you were fishing for any kind of trout other than browns this is where you want to focus your efforts. The only two times brown trout aggressively utilize this portion of a lake is for the occasional quick feeding or an ill-fated spawning attempt. These areas usually have light backgrounds causing a brown trout a feeling of insecurity. As a result, feeding during the day is brief and the majority of the feeding time spent in this area occurs under the cover of darkness. Spawning is the only urge that can totally overcome a brown trout enough to be seen in the littoral zone during the day. Browns will try to spawn in lakes, but without the proper sized substrate and water velocity of a river most all attempts are futile. When feeding in this zone, experience teaches us browns are mainly interested in either smaller forage fish or the freshwater shrimp (arthropods, technically) found to dominate the vegetation at this depth.

The profundal zone is the deepest part of the lake. Very little in the way of production occurs here. Sunlight does not reach this zone and as a result very little oxygen is available. The small amount occasionally available is usually used by decaying organic (detritus) matter. This zone is neither a good place for brown trout nor the pursuant fly fisherman's flies.

The lake zone most productive for brown trout is the pelagic. This area in a lake is supported on top of the profundal and bordered by the littoral on either side. It should be noted, although sunlight reaches the upper portions of the pelagic zone, production happens at a slower rate than in the littoral zone. Why then do brown trout prefer this region? Part of the answer lies in the aforementioned reason that it is bordered on three of four sides. This creates edges (juxtaposition, if you really want to get technical) brown trout, as predators, favor. For example, a mountain lion would stand a very poor chance of ambushing a mule deer in the large openness of an alfalfa field. However, if the same mule deer were to walk through a narrow, rocky area on the edge of the same field the mountain lion's chances improve dramatically. This same principle applies to brown trout in lakes. Brown trout predation on forage fish usually occurs just inside the pelagic zone where fish just inside the edges of the other areas can be caught off guard. Brown trout cruise these edges from the darkened safety of the lower part of the pelagic zone. The other part of the reason is the pelagic zone is utilized

by larger forage fish for feeding. Forage fish really enjoy feeding on several types of midge (Chironomidae) larvae that inhabit this zone.

Once you are able to compare the horizontal descriptions of the thermal stratification layers with the vertical descriptions of the production zones, you will have a 3-D picture of where to look for brown trout in lakes. The epilimnion is the horizontal temperature layer with the most consistent water temperature, the most biological production and the greatest amount of dissolved oxygen. Of the three choices this is by far the most preferable to the browns.

There are two vertical zones brown trout utilize at different times. The littoral zone is used at night when browns feel their security is not going to be comprised. Also, a small decrease in the very high dissolved oxygen level occurs in this zone at night, making browns more comfortable than during the day. The pelagic zone will be the preferred daytime holding area for the majority of the year.

If you were to mentally divide the lake into horizontal and vertical three-dimensional boxes, the area where the epilimnion and the pelagic zone occupy the same boxes is going to be some of the best producing water during the day. Where the epilimnion and the littoral zone interconnect should be where you are focusing your attention during dusk, dawn and night. This system provides an excellent first step in finding brown trout in lakes. Keeping this in mind let's go ahead and look at a few other factors that also affect brown trout distribution in lakes.

Bed Structure

Aside from temperature and dissolved oxygen the morphology of a lake or pond bed will have the next greatest effect on brown trout distribution. I'm hesitant to use another terrestrial analogy, but this theory you can observe almost anywhere. All that is required is a few horses or cows in a pasture. If you happen to drive by this pasture everyday, so much the better. By watching these animals you will probably notice they are seldom far from some kind of structure of variance in the pasture. It might be a

Wind direction can be a clue as to where you want to start fishing.

Drop-offs are great places to fish for brown trout in lakes.

Inlet channels can sometimes extend into the lake forming good drop-offs to fish.

Drop-offs in lakes are good places to fish.

Inlet channels can be good places to find drop-offs and ledges.

fence, rock or nothing more than a break in terrain. Seldom will you see them either widely separated or very far from some kind of terrain break. Brown trout in lakes behave in a very similar fashion. After locating the correct zones and layers immediately start looking at bed variance.

Drop-Offs

In some texts drop-offs are also referred to as food shelves. Regardless of what you call them they are some of the very best places to locate large browns in lakes. Most drop-offs fit the edge criteria because they are usually the actual boundary between the littoral zone and the pelagic. Drop-offs are easily located. Water color changes from the light reflective tan color of the littoral zone to a dark absorbing blue of the pelagic. Depending on your lake, if you are without a boat, this area can usually be effectively fished either from shore or by wading. Temperature layers will change on drop-offs as well. The optimum water temperature for catching brown trout (56 degrees Fahrenheit to 62 degrees Fahrenheit) in lakes can be found in and around drop-offs. Brown trout also like drop-offs because they change the vertical distribution of a lake's food sources. This provides brown trout with opportunities for many different food sources in a very localized area. The old adage "the more diversified something is the more stable it..." definitely applies here. Brown trout agree with this saying. If your drop-off has a weed bed associated with it, plan on it being one of the most productive fishing areas the lake has to offer. Weed beds provide even more food sources (insects, forage fish, etc..) while the nearby deep water provides the instant safety of cover. Drop-offs usually produce best during midday. When everywhere else on the lake is fishing poor, head for the drop-offs.

Islands and Peninsulas

The water around islands and peninsulas can be a very productive place to fish for brown trout. Like drop-offs, islands and peninsulas create variance in the bed structure, providing holding water for both larvae beds and browns. Peninsulas located on an otherwise barren or smooth shoreline are great places to start fishing a new lake. While fishing these areas work the side of the peninsula the wind is blowing against the longest. Experience has shown brown trout follow the wind, or more accurately, the wind-bound food items around the side of peninsulas. If you learn your lake well enough you will eventually be able to know which side of the peninsula to fish depending on wind direction. The water surrounding islands is usually on a very gentle grade, sloping out toward the middle of the lake. These areas act as large flat food shelves which many larvae beds prefer because the grade makes it very easy for them to get established. The most productive fishing time on waters surrounding islands and peninsulas is in the early morning or late evening.

Stream Inlets and Outlets

Inlets are usually more productive than outlets. If all things were in their "natural" state I'm not sure this would be the case. But, most outlets in brown trout lakes have dams associated with them. If you are permitted to fish along the backside of the dam, do so on very hot unproductive days. Many times the deepest part of the lake is right along the dam. This is one of the easiest places for a fly fisherman to sink a fly into this deep cool water. Stream inlets offer quite a few more options and therefore are more productive.

Stream inlets provide freshly-oxygenated water, food items and usually a cooler water temperature on the side of the lake they enter. If you are fishing from a boat or a float tube be sure to locate the course of the old streambed in the reservoir. These channels can be very productive all year long. Make sure to pay special attention to them during early spring and late fall. Knowing where these underwater channels are can save many fishless days.

Just how important inlet streams of lakes can be to brown trout fishermen in the fall was pressed home to me

quite a few years ago. In an earlier chapter I questioned fishing over spawning brown trout. So as not to appear repugnant it is important you are aware the following experience occurred prior to my current opinion. In fact, it was an influencing factor.

While attending college a friend and I were made privy to a little known stream connecting two lakes in Yellowstone National Park. Further inquiry revealed a group of older fly fishermen who, "used to fish there all the time, but haven't been in there in years." They all told us it should still be great fishing for spawning brown trout

in the fall. The channel, as it is called, started to have something of a mystical quality surrounding it. We soon noticed it was only talked about in hushed tones after furtive sideways glances in either direction. It seemed every extra large brown trout mount gracing a fly shop wall in West Yellowstone originated there.

The channel could only be reached by a boat without a motor. Regulations and rumored high winds on the lower lake, which we needed to cross, convinced us a canoe would be the craft of choice. We found a canoe, bought maps, tied flies, sorted food and agreed on four days that

GUIDO RAHR

wouldn't wreck us academically. A week prior to our scheduled departure there was a notice in the newspaper announcing the U.S. Fish and Wildlife Service decided to close the channel for study purposes. After calling around I found out the channel suddenly had been mysteriously reopened. The trip was on.

The early morning paddle across the lower lake was uneventful. No wind, and better yet nobody, was in sight. After we located the channel we started to walk our boat upstream. The further we walked the more colors appeared on the streambed's larger rocks. Bright reds, yel-

lows, silvers and greens all became visible. It turned out the joke was on us. While most fishermen on the Montana side of Yellowstone had never heard of this "secret spot", it soon became apparent most in Wyoming had. Large numbers of anglers had preceded us in dragging their canoes over the same rocks to create, what my partner called, "the psychedelic streambed."

But aside from the crowds, and more to the point, the spawning browns were truly a sight to behold. The upper channel was wide, shallow and had the perfect sized substrate for spawning. Browns of all different sizes and shapes were packed fin to fin. They were amazing. Spawning sockeye salmon in Alaska remain the only thing I have ever seen equaling the sheer numbers of brown trout we observed. Not wishing to join the other anglers on the bank we quickly caught and released a few trout, took a few photos and headed back downstream. Fortunately the afternoon wind hadn't picked up and we were able to make it back across the lake to a designated campsite for the evening.

While the channel was too crowded for me to really enjoy the angling, it encouraged (forced?) me to start looking for similar situations. I'm happy to report I've found several. They are even better because few people know about them, and this allows me to fish them several days, before the spawning begins each year.

Other Places

So far we have examined where temperatures, zones and holding areas can all be found together. These things will focus the brown trout in any lake. To finish this properly we must look at a few more conditions experience shows brown trout favor. Keep in mind these structures will almost always occur in the parameters we have already examined.

Of those left a good long rocky shoreline is more consistent than the others. Insects adhere to rocks on shorelines and provide an excellent forage base for browns. In addition to this if the rocks are large, angular and blocky, browns might be in the vicinity waiting for fry and baitfish. Larger angular rocks, when tossed in a pile, create pockets smaller fish use for protection. The size of the pockets associated with this type of rock tends to be prejudiced against larger predatory browns, but many smaller ones may be present. Another good place to look for browns is under any kind of natural or unnatural overhead cover. These things can be trees which have fallen into the lake or even an old discarded piece of farm machinery somebody has tossed in. But, just as in rivers and streams submerged overhead cover will hold more brown trout than exposed overhead cover. Regardless of the medium, direct exposure to the surface makes brown trout nervous.

As a last note on where to find browns in lakes never pass up the opportunity to fish over a weed bed. Weed beds act exactly like rocky shorelines and bank structure combined. Submergent and emergent aquatic vegetation provide both food and habitat for trout and their prey.

Brown Trout Lake Behavior

Fooling a brown trout in a lake environment remains one of the most difficult feats in fly fishing. When a temporarily defeated brown breaks the lake's surface and slides to hand the whole experience seems capable of absolving you from all past sins. There are few other angling moments which will provide this much satisfaction.

For this situation to occur with any regularity lake

Lake-caught brown fooled by a streamer.

habits of brown trout must be understood, or at the very least acknowledged. Unlike river-dwelling browns those in lakes are the toughest to catch between mid-June and September. These months are usually associated with the highest daytime temperatures of the year. While these temperatures play a small role in the reluctance of browns to take a fly during this time period, they are definitely not the sole factor. Studies in England have compared seasonal catchability of browns to rainbows. Rainbows, which are less tolerant of high water temperatures than browns, are caught in abundance during the summer months. This leaves photoperiod serving as the explanation.

Photoperiod is simply the amount of daylight in any given 24 hour period that is best suited for growth and maturation. Photoperiod in the summer months is at its greatest amount for the year. Not only is there more light, the intensity of this light is at a high point as well. It is this light intensity that drives browns to impractical depths for the fly fisher. If the fly fisherman is going to catch browns from a lake during these months he should focus his outings early in the morning or at dusk. Night fishing during summer months, which will be covered in another chapter, is also a very viable option.

Let's assume you are going to concentrate your lake angling efforts throughout the remaining eight productive months of the year. Brown trout during this period exhibit two distinct types of travel patterns. The first group exhibits movement only in locally restricted areas. This group will be of average size (10 inches to 21 inches) for the lake and will comprise the majority of the brown trout population. It is browns from this group the fly angler will hook most often. While daily activity will be random, it will always occur in the localized areas. These areas stay consistent and can be found by applying the earlier information in this chapter.

From mid-September on these browns will be found down to 30 feet in depth, while in the winter time the deepest you will find them is about 10 feet. While these depths require the use of a fast sinking specialty line, they can be reached by the fly fisherman. Another positive aspect of this time period for fishing lakes is that browns primarily move during the day. There is no need to stay out all night in order to catch them.

The second travel pattern is usually associated with browns over 21 inches in length. These are the lake dwelling browns a fly angler seldom hooks or, even more rarely, lands. Occasions when the two do get together are usually chronicled by an outdoor magazine offering "Exclusive Photos Of New World Record Brown Trout." Reasons for the scarcity of this event are these large fish are mainly piscivorous and their movements and areas are strictly random. There is no localized area which can be consistently counted on.

If the lakes you fish are thermally stratified pay close attention to the water temperature. Brown trout in these lakes prefer a water temperature of 57 degrees Fahrenheit. At any time or depth you locate this water temperature be sure to spend some time fishing in this zone.

Across the Puddle

Fly fishing for brown trout in lakes and ponds started, across the Atlantic, in Scottish lochs. Early attempts were carried out with fly tackle designed for either Atlantic salmon or sea trout. Spey rods were usually rigged with large tube flies—and still-water brown trout fishing was born. World Wars and industrialization helped the southern spread of still-waters to the rest of Britain. Wars require great amounts of water, and industrialization needs gravel for concrete. Many reservoirs were excavated to fulfill both needs.

When it comes to brown trout fishing in rivers and streams the British have little left to teach us except history. This can be directly attributed to national laws governing resource ownership. Streams and rivers can be privately owned and locked up. Reservoirs, on the other hand, while privately owned, are required by the government to be open to the public. Reservoir owners have viewed this as an opportunity to help their bottom line. This has created a competing "country club" type atmosphere, with each reservoir owner trying to better the competing "club" next door. This system has kept fees (called rod tickets) low, while maintaining a very high level of service. As with private water in the United States rod fees vary, but the average price of a day ticket seems to be around $36 which allows you to keep up to four fish.

Now, if you are starting to compare this system to the United States "U-pay trout farms", please don't. These places don't have cigar smoking old geezers in Bermuda shorts, who pass out cans of corn niblets, cane poles and say they will see you at the scales before you leave. It is true most of these reservoirs have their own hatcheries and stock fish frequently, bear in mind most of these reser-

voirs are well over 100 surface acres in size. Some of the better ones have started releasing fish enough days in advance to ensure some of them will revert back to their natural diet. Studies in Britain have indicated this process, at a minimum, requires 21 days. Studies in the United States appear to back this up revealing no significant difference in spatial distribution and diet between wild fish and those reared in, and released from, a hatchery.

Most of these reservoirs have their own manager. These managers, if they excel at providing good sport, are often followed from reservoir to reservoir, like a discerning clientele follows a great chef. The whole situation has transformed brown trout lake fishing to almost a golf course atmosphere. This provides angling opportunities for those who otherwise would have little hope of affording it. The last directory I saw listed over 650 different reservoirs from which to choose. Species available were listed right next to the maximum size of fly hook allowed. A size eight was the largest I could find. I mention this system not to cheapen the stillwater brown trout fisheries in the United States,

Occasionally you can connect with a lake brown over 21 inches.

but rather to point out possibilities for areas where no brown trout fishing currently exists. Have you ever driven along the interstate through the Midwest and noticed all the borrow pit lakes excavated for the sole purpose of building an overpass? Most of these were excavated deep enough to expose high quality ground water. Right now most of them look pretty stark, but add a few trees, maybe a small shelter, spread the cost among some like-minded friends…give it some thought.

Lake fishing for brown trout is definitely tougher than pursuing them in streams, and as a result it has a few more hard won awards to offer. Study the lakes you intend to fish most often unlike anything you have ever studied in your life. It will require time, patience and the sacrifice of many fishless initial trips. The benefit is once you have mastered the learning curve, large brown trout can be consistently taken on the fly. And there is little better than that.

CHAPTER FOUR

BROWN TROUT AND NYMPH FISHING

Early History

Fly fishing history tends to be a little mundane when compared to its other pursuits. The fun part is, however, that there is a relatively few number of people who can be credited with bringing the sport to its current state.

The man who played an early active role in the imitating of insects for fly fishing was none other than Robert Barnwell Roosevelt. He authored several books on the subject and completed the leg work for a series of people who would follow. Names that bear mentioning are Hewitt, Elizabeth Benjamin, Sara McBride, Mary Orvis Marbury and John Harrington Keene. G.E.M. Skues, who is still known as the father of nymph fishing, did his research across the puddle independently of Roosevelt, and made huge strides toward our current techniques. Skues' first book, published in 1910, *Minor Tactics of the Chalk Stream* includes thirty years of nymph fishing for brown trout as research.

A brown trout's diet is comprised mostly of nymphs.

A fly fisher by the name of Louis Rhead, however, probably deserves credit for bringing nymph fishing to American waters. He could also be credited with being one of the early "publicity anglers." He was quite a marketing man and for several years you could purchase his signature flies from William Mills in New York. As part of this publicity he started writing nymph fishing articles for *Forest and Stream* in the early 1920s. Rhead was also quite the artist, lavishly illustrating these articles with pen and ink drawings. These articles gave modern nymphing its start.

There is not an another brown trout angling technique which is as deadly as the nymph. Year in and year out this is the bread and butter method for the serious brown trout angler. If there is another fly fishing method browns are more vulnerable to than nymphs, I would pay to find out what it is. You have probably guessed by now this is my preferred angling technique for brown trout. As a result of this I have formed stronger opinions (some would say extremely strong) on nymph fishing than any other of the three disciplines (nymph, streamer and dry) I currently use.

Basic Knowledge

I had the good fortune of cutting my teeth on nymph fishing in the hands of an expert and refining it with a maniac. College, while not doing much for my grades, improved my angling technique better than any time period since. A large part of this was directly attributed to Mike Conley. He is one extraordinary nymph fisherman, as anyone who has ever fished with him can attest. Very few people can match his efficiency at nymphing a run. He is the only person I've ever seen consistently catch five or six browns at every run he fishes. Mike still has this raw talent with nymphs that remains unequaled. His ability expands beyond the norm, almost stretching into the sublime. It was under his tutelage I first realized how deadly nymph fishing for brown trout could be. It was from him I first learned about selection, drift and presentation.

Fittingly, my first trout on a nymph was a brown. The fish took a #16 Hare's Ear. Also at the risk of exposing the stream I will tell you it is just outside the city limits of Bozeman, Montana and the fish was holding right next to an old car body the adjoining land owner had placed for erosion control. The indicator system I was using at the time consisted of a small greased piece of fluorescent orange chenille. It vanished so decisively from the water's surface it had to be a take. After setting the hook there was little doubt left in my mind about the brown trout's commitment to nymphs.

This begs the question of what a brown trout nymph fisherman should know. Similar to the early nymph pioneers modern brown trout fishermen face similar obstacles when it comes to gathering regional information. Good brown trout nymph fishing information is best obtained first hand. At the very least, a basic regional knowledge of the larval life that is available to the browns you wish to fish for should be committed to memory. By this I don't necessarily mean taking an entomology class, but rather paying attention to insect size and color. The presentation speed at which the current delivers the nymph is usually so fast a feeding brown has only a brief window of opportunity to decide if it is going to take or not. Contrary to popular opinion size and color are far more important than an exact imitation of the natural insect. Al Troth, a nymph fisherman who needs no introduction, once wrote: "I fish too much to spend a lot of time on slavish imitations. I have taken photographs of a live nymph and an artificial in the water, and when the slides were projected and thrown slightly out of focus, just enough to make it difficult to tell the natural from the copy, the fly imitation usually appeared larger than the natural. This is an indication that a smaller sparsely tied fly would look more lifelike. As a result, the small nymphs I use are simply tied and very sparse." Truer words about nymph fishing for brown trout have never been written.

Following size and color, times of high larval activity and seasonal movement are the next most important factor. If you really want to study, my recommendation would be to learn limiting factors like anchor ice and temperature extremes. Both of these can severely inhibit larval populations, but if you only fish an area in the summer you would not necessarily be aware of their presence. If a brown trout angler learns nothing more than these basics, nymph fishing will become very easy. If you couple these with a pattern selection and some basic technique you should be readily able to catch browns year-round.

To aid in simplifying this let's briefly examine a year on my home waters of southwestern Montana. January and February would probably find you using a larval midge imitation. A Serendipity, Palomino Midge or a Pheasant-Tail Nymph would all be logical choices. These are small flies best imitated on hook sizes #16 and smaller. Popular

You can catch most brown trout with approximately 24 different nymph patterns.

colors are, respectively, bright green, beige and natural pheasant-tail. As the warm weather turns the rivers to spring, caddis and stonefly nymphs start to join the menu. For the caddis, Prince Nymphs, Gold-Ribbed Hare's Ears and the LaFontaine Emergers are tough to beat. Hook sizes from #12 down to about a #16 are justified. Color varies, but a standard dark brown/gray Hare's-Ear and a green Antron emerger works well. The natural peacock used in the Prince is always a great producer. Stoneflies are large and black and best imitated on #2 through #6 hooks. Faithful patterns include Red Bellies, Bitch Creeks and the Troth Stonefly Nymph. Summer will find most of these plus mayflies. Mayflies usually have many regional variations, and a standard nymph pattern from white to dark brown tied on a #14 or smaller hook fits the bill. While this is by no means a complete list it should give you a basic idea of what to look for when gathering nymphing information, and a fly selection for your area.

I've noticed nymph selection seems to travel distinct stages. In the beginning you won't have any faith in nymphs or their ability to produce fish because you have not spent the proper time needed to learn how to fish them effectively. Over time, a few of the more popular patterns will find their way into one of your fly boxes, if for no other reason than you think you need to carry at least a few to feel complete. The third stage will occur after you discover the damn things are actually capable of catching fish. At this point you start to tie all the patterns you can find, imagine or hallucinate about. You'll tie nymphs for hatches you have heard only occur on the other end of the nation; a larval nymph fisherman's paranoia of getting caught short. Pure naked greed is used to accurately describe this accumulation. The final stage is nymph bulimia which usually occurs after the realization you have only used about two dozen patterns out of the six huge fly boxes full of nymphs you have packed around for the previous two years. Final onslaught of this stage finds you giving away most all of the nymphs you never use to friends, local T.U. auctions, etc. This completed, you finally settle on a more or less rational two dozen nymph patterns that you not only have all the faith in the world in, but you use regularly.

Nymph Rods

One of the easiest pieces of nymphing equipment to write about is the fly rod. Recently, fly rod manufacturers, in conjunction with technology, have perfected rods for almost every imaginable fly fishing micro-discipline available, but they have yet to hit upon the perfect nymph rod. Although they are rapidly closing in I'm afraid it will be a few years before they find the combination which will really be suitable. And this is assuming the problem can actually be solved. A perfect nymphing rod action for brown trout requires a contradictory function. Length versus stiffness. Very little doubt exists in my mind that catch rates while using nymphs would probably double if these two properties could ever be married. Successful nymphing for brown trout is a matter of covering as much productive water as possible in the course of a day. Rods longer than nine feet in length are the most efficient at this. Not only can you cast further with less effort, 10 and 11 foot rods will allow you to control and mend almost double the line of a nine foot rod. As with everything in life there are trade-offs.

Anyone who has ever been in a position to observe nymphing browns will tell you success is keyed, among other things, to reaction time. A nymphing brown trout can take and discard a fly so quickly you wonder how many browns we actually catch, as opposed to the number which hook themselves. Once while guiding a fairly adept angler, I had him fish a run in the morning; (the proper time for this run) the sun illuminated the nymphing browns just a few feet away, while we remained in the shadows. He was using an indicator and had managed several takes, but failed to hook them. The problem was his soft-actioned rod. I could see individual fish take the nymph and then discard it, before the client could get his long flimsy rod to the "meat" portion of the action to set the hook. Finally I took to yelling "pull" when the brown would first open its mouth and he was then able to catch several. A portion of this problem would not have existed if the client's reaction time had been a little quicker, but a stiffer rod action would also have compensated for some of this. Here's the trade off: long rods (over 10 feet in length) which are great for casting and line control are too soft for setting the hook in the necessary period of time. For this reason I have yet to see a rod over nine feet I would consider using as a primary nymph rod. Even with the third generation graphites, they seem to lose stiffness dramatically when constructed over nine feet in length. This only starts to change when rods increase in line size. If a company could construct a 10 1/2 foot rod for a number six line which performed like a rod of the same length designed to cast a number nine line the problem would be solved. And while we're in this theoretical design mode let's keep rod weight at or below

2 13/16 ounces for casting an honest 12 hour fishing day without fatigue.

Handles on nymph rods are another area where a need for contradictory designs arises. Factory grips are way too fat most of the time. They could stand to be reduced by half. A smaller grip allows for more precise casting, a better feel and some would say less forearm fatigue during a long day. A long-time angling companion of mine, who builds his own rods, shaves the grips on his nymph rod down to almost nothing and I'll be the first to admit they are comfortable. The only problem with them is when fishing requires the use of a heavy nymph. If you cast a fully weighted number 2 Bitch Creek Nymphs with an additional 10 grains of lead on your leader, and

Fred Kratz hooked up on the Green River in Utah. This brown fell for a size 12 Prince Nymph.

when you add the friction of the water's surface tension, cast after cast, during a 10 hour day on the river the formation of the grip favors the larger one. When you cast this amount of weight there is a tremendous amount of torque created and a smaller grip will focus this pressure on a smaller area of your casting hand rather than spreading it out.

As far as reel seats on nymph rods go I'm a big fan of the downlocking kind. When I'm working over nymphing fish I tend to get excited and my casting form goes to hell. This usually finds me applying more pressure than necessary to the cast, which in turn causes the line coming off the reel to jump and wrap around the butt of the rod. A downlocking reel seat will usually prevent this; an uplocking reel seat seems to catch this loop every time.

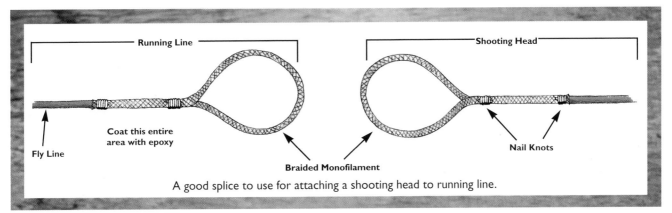

A good splice to use for attaching a shooting head to running line.

Unfortunately I didn't learn to cast from an instructor, so I'm probably stuck with this option.

In the end, a perfect contemporary production nymph rod is made of third generation graphite for a number six line and is nine feet in length. The handle will be a little fatter than necessary, unless you are building one from scratch, then you can make it as skinny as you want. The reel seat will be downlocking, unless you are an expert caster who never gets rattled when faced with voraciously nymphing browns just a few feet away. Just the thought of this makes you quiver. Doesn't it?

Nymphing Lines

Fly lines devoted strictly to nymphing seem to be overlooked. While they play a very important role in the process, the only lines "marketed" as nymph lines are really better suited for streamer fishing. One of the biggest fallacies in nymph fishing for brown trout remains the depth at which to do it. Studies in New Zealand indicate preferred depth for nymphing browns in freestone streams is 3 1/3 feet, and the most common between 2 1/4 and 2 3/4 feet. All of these depths can be readily reached with a floating line. Not only are sinking lines unnecessary 95 percent of the time it is impossible to get good nymph presentation while using them. Bear in mind nymphing is the only technique that uses the subsurface flow of the current to present the fly. How this current is utilized in fly presentation will determine the degree of attractiveness the nymph will have to waiting (feeding) brown trout. Sinking lines simply go too deep and get tangled in currents which you can't control from the surface. One of the keys to proper nymph presentation is the buoyancy of a floating line. To help facilitate this I'll even cut five to seven feet from the front of a weight-forward floating line. After the clipped end of the line is properly sealed, (melt the outside coating of the end with a lighter) this will allow you to attach a leader to the thickest part of a fly line taper. Weight-forward floating lines will successfully present the nymph in well over 90 percent of all brown trout nymphing situations. It should probably be stated I have very little use for any taper (for any purpose) other than the weight-forward variety. The only exception to this I can currently think of is for two-handed Spey casting, where I either prefer a continuous or double-taper line. Double-taper lines, for any other application, are really a false economy. I've never seen a situation where after one taper wore out, the other one was just as badly bleached, cracked and pig-tailed as the first. On top of all this they make it almost impossible to easily handle any kind of wind.

Shooting heads can certainly be a boon to the serious brown trout nymph fisherman. One distinct advantage is they are cheaper. As of this writing a floating shooting head sells for about $20.00, and a regular weight-forward floating fly line costs around $40.00. As prices continue to soar I'm sure this will become a major factor in the choice between the two. Dr. J.M. Conley, the angling mentor whom I have learned far more from than I'll probably ever realize, makes his running lines from old floating lines. From the front (leader and fly end) of a weight-forward fly line, the line's taper extends back about 38 1/2 feet. This measurement will vary a little between manufacturers, but it is pretty easy to see where the other end of the taper connects with the constant diameter line, which in turn forms the remainder of the line. Dr. Conley cuts the worn front taper from the constant diameter line, and uses the latter to form the running line for his newly purchased floating shooting head. Come to think of it, I've witnessed several "full line" devotees (including myself) giving worn out floating lines to him for use as running lines. It's a very functional and inexpensive way to go, and I've included a sketch on how to make a splice to join the two pieces.

Problems with this seemingly low cost alternative are ones of control. While the splice diagram provided is one of the strongest and stiffest for trout fishing, I am of the opinion it causes the line to hinge. This hinged action causes a small loss of control and casting accuracy not unlike a sink-tip line does for streamer fishing. As you will see in a moment, while nymphing requires a hinge in the leader assembly this same hinge in the middle of your fly line makes it difficult to cast accurately. Another accuracy problem is after the shooting head leaves the tip-top of your rod, adjustments or corrections are impossible. For this reason shooting heads lack the inherent accuracy of a full length weight-forward line. Shooting heads also tend to promote using too much line. Even though you know you should really strip more line in before your next cast, you are constantly trying to shortcut this, soon finding yourself trying to handle way more than is accurate. While these are very small gripes, ultimately you should try both and make up your own mind on the cost versus performance aspect.

Indicators, Leaders and Tippets

Without a doubt the device responsible for more browns being caught with nymphs than ever before has to be the strike indicator. Indicators, usually referred to as "bobbers" by non-users, come in all designs, shapes, colors and sizes. If you haven't already noticed, if designed and used properly, I'm a firm believer in strike indicators. Since indicators make a very difficult aspect of the sport more fun and less punishment they get my vote. Please notice this sentence was qualified earlier by the indicators being designed and used properly. Of all the thousands of fly fishing articles that have been written about terminal nymph rigs it absolutely amazes me the amount of advice and the number of theories presented as fact when it is blatantly obvious they have never been tested on the water. The following three rules of terminal nymph rigs have been proven across the world, by different anglers, on almost every type of game fish which will strike a fly presented in the dead-drift manner. All three rules are based on the rudimentary assumption that a dead-drift is the best presentation for nymphing.

The Three Rules of Terminal Nymph Rigs

1. The indicator must be large enough to fully float/support the fly and weight being used.

2. To present a nymph pattern properly the leader must hinge directly in front (fly side) of the indicator.

3. The difference between pressure (force) applied to a piece of monofilament by a river's surface versus the pressure applied to the same piece of monofilament at the same time by a river's streambed is so small it will not affect a dead drift presentation.

If your indicator is not large enough to fully float the fly you are using the result will be a nymph rig which is impossible to achieve a dead-drift presentation with. If your fly of choice continues to "pull under" your indicator increase the size of the indicator until this is solved. Don't worry about "spooking" fish. I've used an indicator which is about five inches long and the same diameter as a cigar—it does not spook fish. In nymphing situations, over 90 percent of the time, feeding fish are usually spooked by someone who blunders across the riffle before he/she even looks to see if any fish are present. Even as you read this you're probably thinking, "yeah well, a large indicator wouldn't work on XYZ creek…" Don't flatter yourself, this system was developed over some of the spookiest browns in the world. Indicator color seems to make no difference either, so pick one you can see easily. Hot pink or yellow

work well in high light conditions, while black or dark blue are optimum for low light.

Of the three rules, the leader which must hinge will probably be the most difficult one for you to accept. Since we were novice fly fishermen we have been taught leaders had to have thick, rigid butt sections. While this is certainly the case for easier casting it is a hindrance for nymph presentation. So-called "nymph leaders" with stiff butt sections tend to keep the rest of the leader and the fly on or near the surface. If the leader is hinged, after the strike indicator, with a knot, loop to loop junction, etc. it will allow the rest of the leader and fly to dangle below the water's surface. Even using a lighter piece of monofilament for a small butt section will aid in presentation. This system is designed around fish catching qualities not casting qualities, so don't get hung up on the latter. Casting quality diminishes quickly once you attach indicator, weight and a heavy nymph. By this I mean it's not pretty, but it still will cast without constantly getting tangled.

It is a known fact that water on a river's surface exerts more pressure than water next to the streambed. This is usually the hydrologic rule which precedes an extremely complex tapered nymph leader formula. While the hydrology is correct, the reasoning for a tapered leader is not. The difference between these two pressures is not great enough to have any bearing whatsoever on fly presentation. Only different current speeds on the surface which attack the leader at the same time (a k a drag) will affect fly presentation. Nymph fishing is difficult enough with-

David Freeman releasing a nice brown trout caught on a size 16 Hare's Ear.

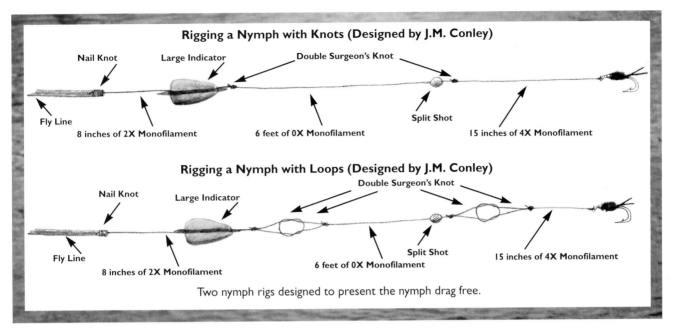

Rigging a Nymph with Knots (Designed by J.M. Conley)

Nail Knot · Large Indicator · Double Surgeon's Knot · Split Shot

Fly Line · 8 inches of 2X Monofilament · 6 feet of 0X Monofilament · 15 inches of 4X Monofilament

Rigging a Nymph with Loops (Designed by J.M. Conley)

Double Surgeon's Knot · Nail Knot · Large Indicator · Split Shot

Fly Line · 8 inches of 2X Monofilament · 6 feet of 0X Monofilament · 15 inches of 4X Monofilament

Two nymph rigs designed to present the nymph drag free.

out trying to cure non-ailments. Nymph fishing for brown trout (strictly freshwater) should never require anything more than a six foot piece of 0X monofilament for the main part of the leader. No taper, no knots, no hassles, just a straight piece of 0X. What should vary is the diameter of the tippet, which is tied to the end of the 0X leader. Tippet length should be around 15 inches, but diameter depends on the conditions in which the browns are feeding. Faster, heavier water allows you to get by with thicker tippets, where slow or extremely shallow water forces tippet sizes smaller than 4X.

The illustration shows two terminal nymph rigs which work well, but apply your own ingenuity to the three rules of terminal nymph rigs and see where it leads.

Weight

More often than not successful nymph fishing for browns requires the use of some weight, other than the fly, attached to your leader. If you happen to fish nothing but very shallow riffles in spring creeks then you can probably safely ignore this section. Otherwise read on.

Applying weight to the leader/tippet combination has driven far more nymph fishermen away than it has converted. It definitely makes casting more difficult. One of the keys to casting with lead is to never use any more than is absolutely necessary. My good friend and angling mentor Dr. J.M. Conley has arrived at 10 grains (one large split shot) as the perfect amount for over 90 percent of the nymphing situations the brown trout angler will encounter. How did he arrive at this amount? Simply through trial and error over thousands of both hours and browns landed. I can attest he is correct. Very, very rarely do I get the feeling the fish are in a lie deeper than my presentation and add additional lead to the leader. When this does happen I'll usually add an additional 15 grains (one extra large split shot). Almost never does this produce more browns than those which were already nymphed out of the run, but it

will occasionally make you feel better before moving on.

As you can see in the illustration the weight is placed directly above the knot which attaches the tippet to the leader. Yes, this makes casting difficult, but remember, successful nymph rigs diminish casting qualities anyway, bringing us to a final key point in using weight. Casting with a weighted terminal rig is damn tough, and occasionally you are going to get so tangled you are money ahead by cutting the whole mess off and tying on fresh. This happens to everybody and there is no way around it. The advice: accept the fact this is going to occur every now and again and make sure it doesn't ruin your day; it's nymph fishing.

Fly Reels For Nymphing

Technology has probably changed fly reels more than any other piece of equipment for nymphing. Disc drags, which on the whole are probably overkill, have been wonderful for handling large browns nymphing in heavy water. You can now not only hook these fish but stand an actual chance of landing them as well. Aside from smoothness and durability the big thing to look for in a good nymph fishing reel is the diameter. Current trends appear to be headed toward wider, smaller diameter reels, with the emphasis placed on greater line capacity. While this is well intentioned, I have guided too many clients that have lost large browns when the fish made runs either directly at them or changed direction abruptly. These smaller diameter reels are incapable of being cranked fast enough to pick up the amount of line needed to stay with a large brown. If a reel's primary use will be on your nymph rod look for one which has a diameter of at least 3-1/4 inches. Nymph fishing for large browns is very hard on the equipment used. One way to protect both fly line and reel is to purchase a reel where the off-side is not perforated. Perforated reels are a carry-over from the days of silk lines which needed drying and thick heavy reel material

David Freeman waiting to net a brown.

tions. First, a rod over ten feet in length is going to do nothing but help you, and secondly always carry a uniform full-sinking line along with your floater. When you nymph fish lakes there is no mending of the line—just casting and the farther you can cast the more water you'll be able to cover and there's more of a chance fish will see your fly. For far casts out of a float tube your rod should probably be a minimum of ten feet in length.

It has been my experience uniform full-sinking lines take and present the fly under water in a lake on a level plane. A sink-tip for example always presents the fly like it is headed back to the lake's surface (where the floating section of the line is). I have never gotten too hung-up on sink rates but like to carry both an intermediate and a fast sink. Coupled with a floating line they keep you prepared for even the most odd-ball situations.

When it comes to leaders for lake fishing, length is a critical issue. Stay away from any leader under 10 feet in length. Some very successful lake fishermen I know will even stretch this out to fifteen or twenty feet. Longer leaders will give the fly an enticing undulating motion browns seem to like.

Techniques

One of the many neat things about nymph fishing for browns is the endless number of strategies and techniques involved. Some of the most beneficial techniques available to the nymph fisherman can be accomplished with nothing more than the extra movement of the fly rod. Sadly, it is these rod techniques that are most often over-

which needed to be made lighter. Nowadays these perforations just allow sand and dirt onto the fly line and into the gears of the reel.

Except for these few things to watch out for technology has made it increasingly difficult to purchase a truly terrible reel.

Equipment For Nymphing Lakes

Almost all of the advice in the preceding paragraphs is also practical for lake nymphing, with two notable excep-

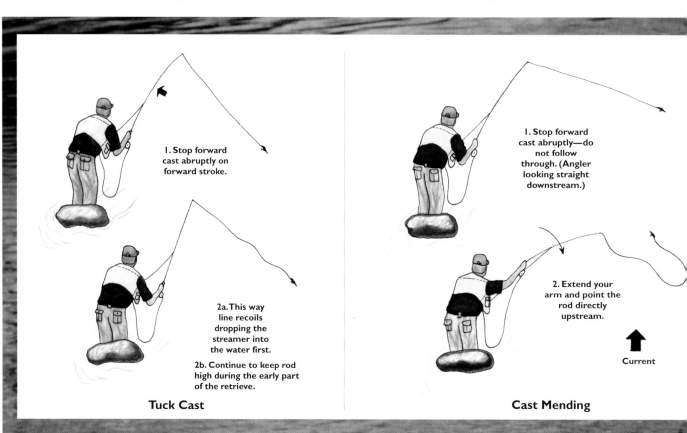

1. Stop forward cast abruptly on forward stroke.

2a. This way line recoils dropping the streamer into the water first.

2b. Continue to keep rod high during the early part of the retrieve.

Tuck Cast

1. Stop forward cast abruptly—do not follow through. (Angler looking straight downstream.)

2. Extend your arm and point the rod directly upstream.

Current

Cast Mending

looked. Years of guiding has allowed me the good fortune to observe many different styles and twists. A few simple extra moves with the fly rod is one of the major differences between an average fly fisherman and a great one. The majority of fly anglers are capable of casting well but have not bothered to apply any additional thought to the many extra advantages that can be gained by modifying their cast.

Tuck Cast

The tuck cast is very easy to execute. Nothing more is required than to stop a regular cast early and abruptly on the forward stroke. Stopping the forward stroke early will cause the stored energy in the cast to recoil the fly line.

The beauty is it allows the fly and any additional weight you have added to your line to enter the water sooner than the fly line. While this may not sound like a major selling point at first, try it with the already recommended terminal rig formula. The tuck cast will prevent the majority of leader tangles associated with nymph fishing.

Allowing the fly to enter the water well before the fly line will also allow the fly to sink very rapidly at the beginning of the drift which ensures it will spend more time at the depth you want. Soft or normal casting for nymph fishing involves too much travel time for the fly; by the time it reaches the right depth the drift is over.

Another reason this cast is so effective for nymph fishing is it allows your fly line to hit the water pre-mended. It virtually eliminates drag in this very early, and crucial, part of the drift. Opposite directional forces on the water's

surface which cause line drag can obviously be overcome by mending, but often drag is encountered between the end of the cast and when you can get to the first mend. By then your line can already be dragging on the surface and no amount of mending will get you caught up.

Cast Mends

This technique can either be used alone or in conjunction with the tuck cast. As with the tuck cast stop the forward cast early and then simply point upstream with your rod arm before the fly line hits the water. This delivers an upstream mend. For a downstream mend just reverse the direction you point your rod arm. It is very simple. When used in conjunction with the tuck cast they can almost eliminate the need for "maintenance" mends during the drift. Having the mend in the cast also provides an economy of motion which is helpful during a long day on the water. It will eliminate a good deal of wasted rod movement.

Single-Handed Spey

In theory this is not really a true Spey cast, but the differences are minute. What the two share is the water's drag on the fly line being used to load the rod. Single-handed Spey casts work well when there is no room for a back cast and the river holds strong, heavy current from bank to bank. You will find this cast tough to master without the heavy current to help load the rod.

With no less than thirty feet of fly line extended past the end of the rod the first step is to simply let the current

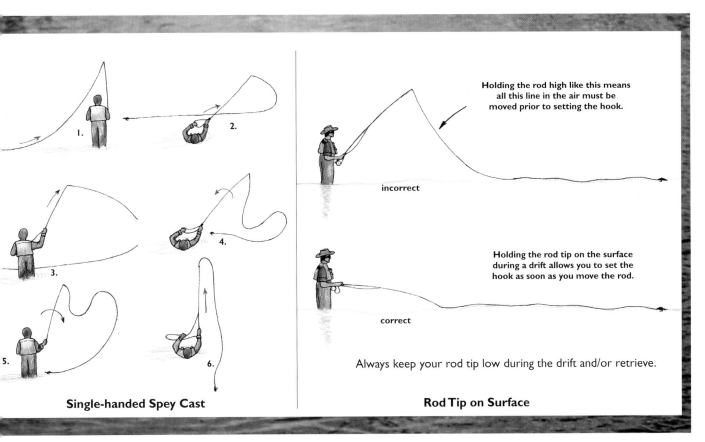

Holding the rod high like this means all this line in the air must be moved prior to setting the hook.

incorrect

Holding the rod tip on the surface during a drift allows you to set the hook as soon as you move the rod.

correct

Always keep your rod tip low during the drift and/or retrieve.

Single-handed Spey Cast

Rod Tip on Surface

drag the line downstream until it is straight. To start the cast, position the tip of the rod on the water's surface pointing downstream toward the extended line. Raise the tip of the rod quickly and then move it directly upstream until the rod crosses your body, with the tip pointing upstream. The line should come skittering directly upstream when this occurs. Now, with an increase in momentum, reverse this motion by moving the rod tip in a half circle, out in front of you, until the rod tip returns to the original raised position. The idea of these two maneuvers is to increase line speed and friction at the same time which will load the rod. Without stopping, cast the rod, like the final part of a roll cast, in the direction you want your cast to land. For all practical purposes this is a single Spey cast performed with a one-handed rod. Newer, stiffer graphite rods make this cast easier than it sounds to perform. The accelerated line speed guarantees farther distances than the traditional roll cast.

Presentation

Now that you have learned three great casts for mending the line, there is one more option; don't mend if you don't have to. If it is at all possible try to present a nymph upstream from your position. Spend the extra time required to get into this position. Not only will this eliminate the need to mend the fly line, the downstream current will work to push your line towards the bottom. With proper mending, cross-stream presentations are very doable but the current will often get "under" the slim side profile of the line and lift it off the bottom. When you cast upstream the current is pushing down on a substantial length of line. Elimination of mending dramatically ,decreases the number of things that can go wrong during a drift and also allows greater concentration on the fishing at hand.

Rod and Line Control

Prosperous nymph fishing for brown trout is a game of split-second timing. All too often good anglers who spend many hours on the water have figured out the correct fly, can cast well and can mend the fly line correctly when required, still fail to catch browns because they hold the tip of their rod waist-high while the nymph completes the drift. As pointed out earlier, if you have ever watched an actively nymphing brown take an imitation you know it does not take long for them to discard it. We only hook these fish when the hook lodges in the corner (the mandible) of their mouth during this rejection. The percentage of hook-ups versus takes will be increased by pulling the line quickly (or setting the hook, whatever you wish to call it) when you first detect the strike. While this sounds very elementary the number of anglers that fail to do this would startle you. Correctly setting the hook while nymph fishing cannot be accomplished if the tip of the fly rod is anywhere but on the surface of the water with only a minimal amount of slack line extending from it. From this position you are immediately tightening line when the rod starts to move.

Otherwise you have to move all the line between the end of the rod and the water before the line in the water begins to tighten.

Keeping the rod tip on or even in, the water's surface also allows you to maximize your hook setting radius. This is the distance between the water's surface and the rod tip, when your rod arm is extended straight overhead. If you hold the rod tip at waist height you are effectively giving away the most powerful part of this radius. It is impossible to generate any power when your rod arm is directly overhead.

Another nymphing secret that will raise your number of hook-ups is to always set the hook with a sweeping motion to the side. When nymph fishing the first move on a strike should never be to raise your rod straight in the air. Most of the time sweeping the rod off to one side or another seems to result in more fish hooked.

After you have cast your nymph upstream the dead-drift presentation will begin. During this drift you will have to pull in slack line as the current feeds the fly over the run and back toward you. How you pull in this line will also dictate success. Let the current dictate how fast you pull it in through the index finger of your rod hand. You want to retrieve the line fast enough to prevent line from piling up in front of the rod tip, but slow enough so you are not disturbing the natural drift of the fly. Strip the line with your off hand and then drop it on the water or whatever surface you happen to be standing on, before reaching back to your rod hand for another strip. Do not worry about fancy hand retrieves or trying to coil the line on the small finger of your rod hand. Pay attention! All these parlor tricks you read about do nothing but allow slack line to develop out in front of the rod tip. Slack will prevent you from setting the hook in time. I would much rather have the loose line at my feet and not miss the strike.

Nymph fishing for brown trout not only provides some of the finest sport available but some of the most productive as well. The techniques put forth in this chapter are really pretty straight forward. Far too many nymph fishing articles have been written on the exact nature of this or the need for only that. Having fallen prey to most of these ideas at one time or another, I am of the opinion only one course of action is worthwhile: concentrate on the basics and keep the nymph rig as simple as possible.

A final recommendation for becoming a successful brown trout nymph fisherman is to find a location where it is possible to observe nymphing fish. The location might be a high bluff, large rock or even a bridge, as long as it provides a clear aerial view of the run and the browns. This will allow you to observe feeding habits as well as how the browns actively use the current to their advantage while feeding. Then present nymphs to these very fish. This will help you recognize and pattern certain situations. This exercise will not only assist you in fishing nymphs but should prove useful in the rest of your brown trout angling as well.

CHAPTER FIVE

STREAMERS

Back Cast

I can't think of another form of fly fishing that brings more pleasurable excitement to the brown trout angler. Streamer fishing has the allure of big fish coupled with a mysterious history. The early streamer patterns are almost impossible to trace. Ernest Schwiebert in Volume II of *Trout* claims the Algoma Indians, who lived in the Canadian Arctic, were possibly the first to lash bucktail to their fishing hooks. Other sources tell us prior to the Algoma, crude wooden hooks with polar bear hair attached to their shanks were discovered along the far northern coast of Alaska. According to yet another tale the first streamer was accidently produced when a dry fly hackle unwound from a poorly constructed fly, causing the hackle to trail behind the main fly body. One book even goes so far as to quote "authentic records." These records (what or wherever they are) proclaim a Mr. Herbert L. Welch of Mooselookmeguntic (I am not making this up), Maine tied the first streamer in 1901. Several different maps failed to show a town in Maine by this name. There is however a Mooselookmeguntic Lake on the Maine-New Hampshire border.

Streamer fishing seemed to muddle along in this confused state for quite some time. Finally in 1935 a gentleman by the name of Preston Jennings seemed to put it all together and published a book titled A *Book Of Trout Flies.* His book was the first to obstinately focus on very exacting minnow imitations and it also seemed to conclude all the streamer development which had occurred at that time.

Around this same time period Western streamer fishing for brown trout was coming into its own. Not only had Dan Bailey already set up shop in Livingston, Montana but Mr. Jennings had already joined him on a fishing trip or two. Some other Montana residents had already start-ed to develop streamers of their own. A gentleman from Missoula named Franz (F.B.) Pott developed woven-bodied wet flies in 1920. These flies were (and still are) fished in a typical down and across streamer fashion. The Pott Hair Fly has accounted for many browns when fished in this fashion.

This tying style was then adopted and made popular by Montana angling legend George Grant of Butte. Here the style in which these flies were fished changed dramatically. Because Grant's home river, the Big Hole, has such a tremendous stonefly population these woven-bodied flies became popular as nymphs and were fished accordingly. Otherwise they probably would have become some of the first brown trout streamers.

Modern brown trout streamer fishing as we know it received its improbable start from a Californian who spent his summers in West Yellowstone. Don Martinez owned a small fly fishing specialty shop in "West" and also invented the original Woolly Worm pattern in the late 1930s. Most all of the long-shanked chenille-bodied streamers that are

MR. PAT BARNES

Don Martinez (center) talking with Pat Barnes in Don's West Yellowstone fly shop.

A nice brown which fell prey to a **Woolly Bugger.**

so popular today owe their origins to this fly. The contribution of the Woolly Worm to today's brown trout streamer fishing is vastly understated. Not only were length and material married for the first time, but I believe this was also one of the first flies to have the hackle palmered over its entire body.

Streamer and Brown Trout Appeal

Nowadays fly fishing in general, and for browns in particular, always seems to focus on exacting imitations, presentation and technique. Streamer fishing, in most all cases, successfully ignores most of this and tends to get right to the heart of the matter. Brown trout eat small fish and when available they will also eat crayfish, sculpin, stonefly nymphs and anything else that looks like it could provide a substantial meal.

One of the best parts of this whole scenario is that brown trout are not that particular over how streamers are presented. Oh sure, there are a few tricks of the trade but as a rule casts can be tossed with reckless abandon, and as long as the fly sinks quickly (in freestone rivers) and the retrieval matches the proper conditions you should eventually be met by a hungry brown.

Many people have asked me what a good streamer river looks like. Without trying to provide a flip answer my response is usually, "one where you catch a lot of trout on streamers." Initially this sounds self-evident, but if you think about it, the answer is one of bare honesty. Of all the streams I've been fortunate enough to fish the Big Hole River in western Montana, for my money, is the quintessential streamer river. The spring colors alone are worth the trip—lime green grass merges with powder blue skies and fast flowing water which has the ability to become a reddish-brown without ever becoming muddy and unfishable. There are two types of stream banks on the Big Hole; ones with brushy overhead cover or banks that are deeply

undercut. Both lend themselves to holding large browns that are just looking for an opportunity to ravage a properly presented streamer pattern.

This river is known for its famous (I'll even go so far as to offer the opinion of occasionally overrated) salmonfly hatch in late spring. This is an excellent time to catch browns with black and blue Electric Buggers, Red Bellied Yuk Bugs and Wool-headed Sculpins. About anything will work as long as it's about the size of a stonefly nymph and black.

While this is the time of year for which the Big Hole is famous, the streamer fishing prior to and after this major event can be very rewarding as well. Sculpin patterns, standard Flash-A-Buggers and Zonkers are all good choices during these "off" or "non-hatch" times. Big Hole substrate is comprised primarily of basketball-sized rocks. They provide a maximum amount of "nooks and crannies" the sculpin and other smaller forage fish use as habitat.

This river is best fished from a drift boat, held slightly off shore, while fishermen launch heavily weighted streamers back toward the bank. Because of the brush and submerged logs this angling method claims its fair share of flies. But it also produces trophy browns. After a day on the Big Hole you never again have to ask what a good streamer river looks like.

Basic Streamer Knowledge

Making knowledgeable streamer selections is far easier than it is with nymphs. Almost all of the small entomological details are removed from the equation. One of my favorite stories illustrating this point is chronicled in Harmon Henkin's book *Fly Tackle*. The story involved two famous angling authors, one of which is none other than Mr. Preston Jennings. The other writer was Ed Zern. Jennings' book *A Book Of Trout Flies* had already been released and earned him the reputation of a master fly

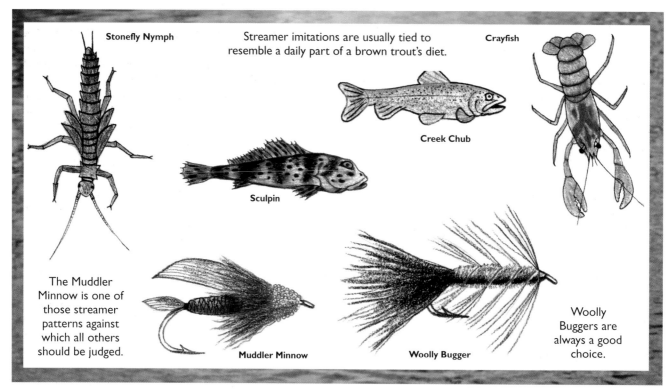

Stonefly Nymph

Streamer imitations are usually tied to resemble a daily part of a brown trout's diet.

Crayfish

Creek Chub

Sculpin

The Muddler Minnow is one of those streamer patterns against which all others should be judged.

Muddler Minnow

Woolly Bugger

Woolly Buggers are always a good choice.

fisherman. Ed Zern a young columnist for *Field & Stream* happened to be at a meeting where Jennings was the keynote speaker. Jennings had apparently gone on ad infinitum about the importance of having the correct minnow imitations for streamer fishing. Finally Zern ran out of patience. He stood up and declared something to the effect of "I don't believe you can tie a streamer pattern that I can't catch a trout on, and furthermore I'm willing to wager anything you'd like!" Jennings left immediately and rumor has it relations between the two stayed strained for many years. As it turns out both men were correct, and there are really only two types of streamers to choose from. There are exacting imitations and those, for lack of a better term, I'll call attractor patterns (the bane of the serious dry fly fisherman).

Imitations are usually tied to resemble a part of a brown trout's diet. Sculpins, crayfish, large stonefly nymphs and general baitfish patterns are all good choices. These imitations can be as complex or as simple as the individual tier chooses. One of my major complaints is the streamer patterns most angling writers design and promote. These exacting imitations are a nightmare to tie and seldom prove durable while fishing. A good rule of thumb when selecting imitation streamer patterns to tie and fish with is what I call the Muddler Minnow Rule. The Muddler is a streamer and possibly one of the greatest flies of all time, developed by Don Gapen for Labrador brook trout. Before I choose a streamer pattern for my fly box I ask the question, "is the fly tougher than a Muddler Minnow to construct and will it prove to be as durable?" If it takes longer to tie than a Muddler then it's not worth fooling with. Anybody with a minimal amount of fly tying skill is capable of tying tougher patterns, but why bother? As far as

imitations go the Muddler is at the top of the tying difficulty versus effectiveness and durability scale. You can certainly find flies with more complex tying instructions, but they won't be any more effective or durable than a Muddler. All of the streamer patterns presented in Chapter 8 have passed this test.

Attractor streamers are fun to tie and fish with because they don't have to make any natural sense to prove effective. These types of streamers are tied in the wildest colors and in various sizes. You can try anything your imagination and skills can manage to lash to the shank of a hook. It's all fair game—well almost, there are some current trends in question.

Streamers (and nymphs) are being tied around a brass bead(s) which is threaded onto the shank of the hook before any fly tying materials are attached. This technique seems to provide good results. Some tiers are even mounting full plastic bodies complete with a plastic diving lip protruding from the front of the "fly". I'm not sure when this ceases to be a fly and becomes a lure. I'm probably more liberal than most, and opinions on this need to remain open. At one point Don Martinez, in a letter describing his fly to Preston Jennings, even labeled the Woolly Worm a lure.

While I don't yet subscribe to all of the patterns and techniques presented, a great example of thought and attractor streamer patterns can be found in Gary LaFontaine's latest book *Trout Flies*. This book presents some streamer patterns and trout behavioral characteristics so bizarre they have to be worth a second look. One thing I wholeheartedly agree with in Gary's book is a taking characteristic of trout which he describes, I will deal with this a little later.

Equipment For Streamer Fishing

Rods

Very few pieces of fly fishing tackle have undergone a change of use the way the streamer rod has. I'll stick with what I said about nymph rods; it can be made out of anything as long as it is graphite—and the 3rd generation graphite is the best in this category. Early rods maintained a slow powerful action which was probably based on a bamboo action. This action remained dominant while materials made the fiberglass to graphite transition. It was the way streamer rods were supposed to be. After giving a slow-actioned rod the "fly shop wiggle" anyone who didn't proclaim it a streamer rod obviously didn't know what they were talking about

Graphite helped stiffen fly rods, but drift boats have done more to change streamer rod action than anything else. A drift boat first made its way east of the Rockies in 1947. Another 40 years or so have passed and it seems this style of boat has almost become more important than the fishing. Where the boat used to be a method of getting from one fishing area to another it has now become part of the angling technique. One of the more popular techniques that evolved in the Rocky Mountain West is holding the floating drift boat about 30 yards away from the bank while both anglers toss streamers toward pockets located on this same bank. The streamers are tied on fully weighted #2 and #4 hooks and are usually accompanied by leaders carrying several large split shot as well.

As you might expect with this type of fishing the more pockets you hit the more fish you are going to catch. To make these repeated quick casts requires an extremely stout rod. Because there is so much weight involved the length of the rod doesn't make a tremendous amount of difference. If this describes the majority of your fishing a good streamer rod should be one which is about 8'6" feet long with the action of a broomhandle. You won't regret this choice for both its performance and durability. Fishing from a drift boat is very tough on fly rods; there are a lot of abrasive surfaces and plenty of sides and seat edges to nick your rod. The newer stiffer rods seem to hold up better.

If you seem to spend the majority of your fishing time using smaller (#6 hooks and down) streamers and long leaders, a 10 foot moderate action rod might be the rod for you. Look around before you buy.

Rod weights for successful streamer fishing can vary considerably. If your streamer fishing falls into the longer tippet/smaller fly category you might be able to get by with a five weight. When casting heavily weighted streamers from a drift boat all day you might want to use an eight weight. My personal all-around streamer rod is a 9'6" long third generation graphite seven weight. It seems to be a good marriage between the large and small rods.

As far as the bells and whistles I think a streamer rod should have them all. Butt extensions are great for resting the weight of your outfit on the underside of your forearm. This aids in taking some of the strain off your wrist.

Aluminum reel seats should be standard because of their durability factor. A note of caution here make sure to check that your reel foot properly fits the rod's seat. I once made the mistake of bringing a new rod and reel (they were marketed by the same manufacturer as a set) to the other side of the world only to have the reel foot not slide into the pocket on the reel seat. Fortunately this was not my client's primary outfit but was a last minute toss in at the request of the manufacturer. I think they now have the problem worked out.

An extra fat full wells grip is a nice handle to have on any large streamer rod. Once again, it disperses the weight evenly to your hand.

If you are going to make your own rod don't be afraid to use guides one size larger than what the specifications call for. For instance, the first stripping guide on the butt section (from the reel) should be 14(mm), followed by a 12(mm). This will allow heavier line sizes to pass cleanly through the guides, which will result in easier and longer casts. This also helps in reducing wear on the stripping guides. Because of the way a rod bends the last guide (closest to the ferrule) the butt section always seems to wear out first. Using larger stripping guides seems to help eliminate this.

Inventing the perfect streamer rod forces us to examine ferrules. If you are going to have only one streamer rod choose one without the internal-spigot type ferrule. They are only superior to the sleeve type for dry fly rods. Internal-spigot ferrules tend to wear very quickly when you are using heavy flies or sink-tip lines. A friend of mine

David Freeman holding a large brown trout.

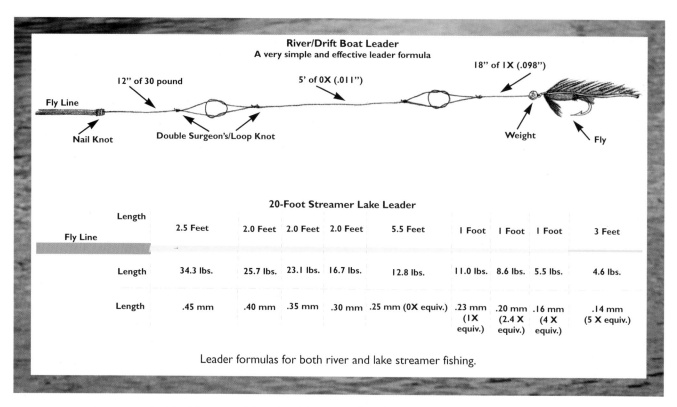

Fly Line	Length								
	2.5 Feet	2.0 Feet	2.0 Feet	2.0 Feet	5.5 Feet	1 Foot	1 Foot	1 Foot	3 Feet
Length	34.3 lbs.	25.7 lbs.	23.1 lbs.	16.7 lbs.	12.8 lbs.	11.0 lbs.	8.6 lbs.	5.5 lbs.	4.6 lbs.
Length	.45 mm	.40 mm	.35 mm	.30 mm	.25 mm (0X equiv.)	.23 mm (1X equiv.)	.20 mm (2.4X equiv.)	.16 mm (4X equiv.)	.14 mm (5X equiv.)

20-Foot Streamer Lake Leader

Leader formulas for both river and lake streamer fishing.

once wore out a new rod with this type of ferrule within one year. Stay away from them.

And oh, by the way...did I mention the perfect streamer rod will not only have all these attributes but shouldn't weigh more than about 3 1/8 ounces?

Lines

Line choice depends on water conditions. For early spring and low-water conditions there isn't much reason to use anything but a floating line. If you plan to use heavy streamers don't use a line weight less than a seven. Anything less than this will not have a large enough diameter to fully support the large fly.

The rest of the year, a sink-tip should be your primary choice and is probably the ultimate streamer line. You will forfeit some line control but will gain access to fish a traditional floating line just can't reach. If most of your streamer fishing for brown trout occurs in heavy freestone rivers don't mess with anything less than a type four sink-tip. The sink rate for this line should be around four to five inches per second. Some faster lines are out there but they are a bear to pick up out of the water. Type fours are more than sufficient, especially if you weight your streamer patterns.

Reels

The key to a good streamer reel is capacity. A good rule of thumb is to purchase the next larger size than the recommended one for the line weight you intend on using. For instance if your goal is to set up a seven weight streamer outfit buy a reel that is rated for an eight or a nine line. This will give you plenty of room for your line and also help to better balance the outfit. Advertised capacities are usu-

ally a far cry from reality. Also look for a reel with a nice large handle. Streamer fishing for browns from a moving drift boat is one way to ensure things happen very quickly. Don't take a chance on losing a big brown because you were fumbling around with a tiny handle. For some reason, probably only known to a production engineer, manufacturers always seem to put a disproportionately small handle on their larger models. If you happen to fall in love with a reel with this problem, however, all is not lost. A friend of mine has taken to slipping small pieces of surgical tubing over small reel handles. It provides a large, inexpensive non-slip grip.

Leaders

For streamer leaders let form follow function. The shorter a leader you can get by with the better off you are going to be. Fishing streamers from a drift boat in a river should never require a leader longer than eight feet. Usually five or six feet will suffice. Save the long complex tapered leaders for lake fishing. In certain situations fishing a 20-foot streamer leader in a lake is the hot ticket. A leader of this length can help give your fly more action. This seems to hold true especially if you are trolling from a float tube, it creates motion brown trout can't resist.

Weight

Another secret for successful streamer fishing is to locate any split shot you are using right above the knot holding the fly to the tippet. Too many anglers pinch their splitshot 12 to 18 inches above the fly. Locating the weight right next to the fly not only causes it to sink faster, giving you a longer drift at the proper depth, but reduces the sling-shot effect which all too often ends in a tangled mess.

Unlike nymph fishing there should be enough terminal weight on your streamer rig to promote this, especially if you are using a sink-tip. Please don't think this will inhibit browns from taking your fly, they simply don't care; worry more about presentation. Hundreds (if not thousands) of browns have been caught in this very manner. Remember the creed for streamer fishing for brown trout: "It just might be impossible to fish a streamer too deep." A good way to find the proper depth is to keep adding weight until you are constantly losing flies on the bottom. Then simply remove the last bit of lead you put on. Yes, this method costs you several flies, but you did say you wanted to catch more browns, didn't you?

Techniques

If there is one word that describes streamer techniques it would have to be: Overlooked. Fishing for browns will require a good portion of your fishing time be spent with a streamer tied on the end of your tippet. Unfortunately, you see anglers who have spent considerable time and money to fish certain rivers, tossing streamers haphazardly in every direction. As I mentioned earlier this style will eventually be met with some success. But why not fish the streamer pattern to its fullest potential? There are some methods for the madness. Here's how.

Don't be afraid to place additional weight right in front of the knot, it causes the fly to sink faster.

Split Shot or "Twist On"

Where to place the weight when fishing a streamer.

The Parallel Drift

Gary LaFontaine has spent more time observing trout looking at flies than anybody else I'm aware of. It should be noted when I say "observing" I mean actually laying on his back on a riverbed, in a rubber suit, while fishing companions pass a myriad of flies over him and the waiting trout. And you thought you were hard-core? While we have never met I have always marveled at some of Gary's theories. In his latest book *Trout Flies*, there is one theory I couldn't agree with more. I knew this streamer technique out-produced all others, but I never knew why. Gary writes: "Trout respond more seriously (grasping instead of nipping) to flies that appear outside the holding area and swim into it rather than vice versa."

Truer words were never written about brown trout streamer fishing. Rainbows tend to use their speed to chase things down, while browns rely on their well evolved predatory patience. Standard routine here in the West is to float by drift boat about 20 or 30 yards from the bank while the fishermen toss and retrieve streamer patterns in a perpendicular fashion toward this same bank. This means most streamer patterns are presented in the least effective manner. Gary's method is easily duplicated from a moving drift boat. While the boat is being rowed parallel to the streambank, cast your fly as close to the bank as you possibly can without getting hung-up. Then, instead of lowering your rod tip and retrieving your fly straight back to the boat take your rod and make either a large upstream or downstream mend. It's your choice and depends on which one you feel the most comfortable in handling.

I prefer to make a downstream mend. This mend requires more adjusting to keep the fly drifting drag free but it seems to have several inherent advantages over the upstream mend. First you have the downstream current pushing the fly line that is actually underwater, down deeper. With an upstream mend the downstream current seems to "lift" the line towards the surface. Second, and probably most important, I feel you avoid losing more flies. The edge of the drift is constantly visible because the floating line marks the downstream progress of the drift. Very often, it is the downstream side of the drift which becomes snagged first. With the upstream mend, the sunken fly is leading the charge into obvious submerged logs and overhanging brush. The fly is always a little closer to getting hung up than you think.

So after all this why would anyone want to use the upstream mend for fishing streamers out of a drift boat? One advantage is it seems to present the fly a little slower. Fly speed plays a very important role, and is one of the first things you should think about changing if the downstream mend isn't producing any takes. Another argument is the first thing the brown trout sees will be the fly; the fish won't have the line passing over its head first and the fly second. A gentleman I have shared countless hours of drift boat streamer fishing with always seems to out-fish me by using an upstream mend. All of the arguments aside I still stand by what I stated earlier; it doesn't seem to make a great deal of difference either way as long as the fly is kept as closely parallel to the bank as long as possible. This is the key. When you are fishing undercut banks from a boat things happen very quickly. The parallel drift maximizes the amount of time your streamer spends in prime brown trout holding water.

Aside from the behavioral characteristics Gary observed, part of the reason this technique is so successful has to do with the comfort zone of the brown trout. Because of the way a brown trout's eyes are constructed they are more efficient looking out from under a dark undercut bank, silhouetting prey against the light background of the open river than looking in toward a dark bank from the light in the middle of the river.

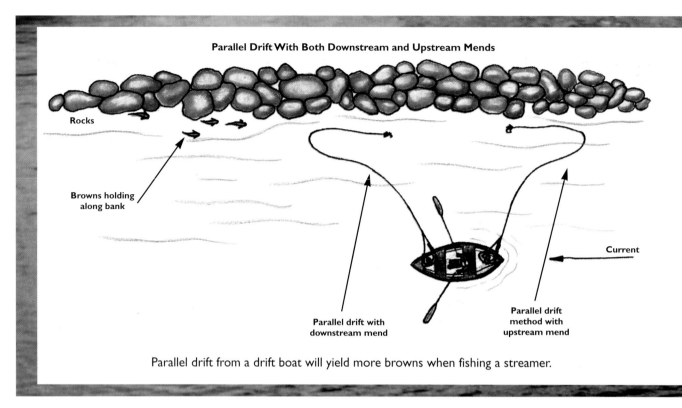

Parallel Drift With Both Downstream and Upstream Mends

Rocks

Browns holding
along bank

Current

Parallel drift with
downstream mend

Parallel drift
method with
upstream mend

Parallel drift from a drift boat will yield more browns when fishing a streamer.

Down and Across

This technique might be the oldest and most proven technique in fly fishing. The number of fish which have been caught using this technique, or subtle variances of it, has to be staggering. Because of this technique's thoroughness if you fish streamers while wading this is the primary technique you should be using. Many different twists and spins have been added to what was initially introduced as greased-line fishing. One distinct advantage of wade-fishing is that you have control over the amount of streamer coverage each fished area receives. The down and across technique allows you to maximize this advantage.

If executed properly, this technique will allow you to prospect a pool in sweeping drifts, each one six to 12 inches longer than the last. When finished with a pool your streamer will have passed through every inch of available holding water. This is a wonderful presentation on those particularly difficult days when brown trout fishing seems to diminish to a matter of not making any mistakes and simply out-persevering the fish.

The first cast should be made just upstream from the pool you want to fish and almost perpendicular to the river. Position yourself so this cast quarters a little bit downstream. You're basically letting the current swing the fly "down and across" so the streamer just passes through the upstream edge of the pool. The next move is to take a small step downstream and complete the same cast again. Sound simple? Good, because this part is. It is what you choose to do with the fly line while it is floating downstream between casts that becomes complicated.

The first move after your fly hits the water should (usually) be a big upstream mend. This will allow two things

to happen. First, it will cause your streamer to swing directly downstream from your fly line, which in turn will cause it to pass through the pool slower.

Secondly, since the pass of the streamer is slowed down it will have more time to sink to a more appropriate depth. Shortly after the drift begins the current will take the initial mend out of your line and another small mend may be needed to maintain consistent fly speed during the rest of the drift. Remember to always make your casts a little longer than what you think is necessary. By the time you put a mend or two into the line it will shorten the streamer's downstream swing.

Sometime between the first mend and the end of the drift you should be able to "track" the swinging fly line with your rod tip. Contrary to what a popular book about this type of streamer presentation says, "tracking" is nothing more than keeping a small amount of constant tension on the line and following the fly line while it completes the rest of its swing. The best way to tell if you are doing this correctly is to have a brown trout hit your streamer. If the brown just taps it and then gets off the hook, you didn't have enough tension on the line and you were not tracking correctly. If the brown hits the fly and your knees buckle from excitement (believe me, it doesn't necessarily take a large fish to cause this) and you seem frozen, unable to do anything but stand there and hang on for a split second, then you have the tension and the tracking about right. Admittedly, this split-second panic becomes an addiction unlike any other I've ever experienced and after a few fish you'll be able to do it right every time. For this reason it is best to fish the drift with a "soft loop" of line between the reel and your index finger.

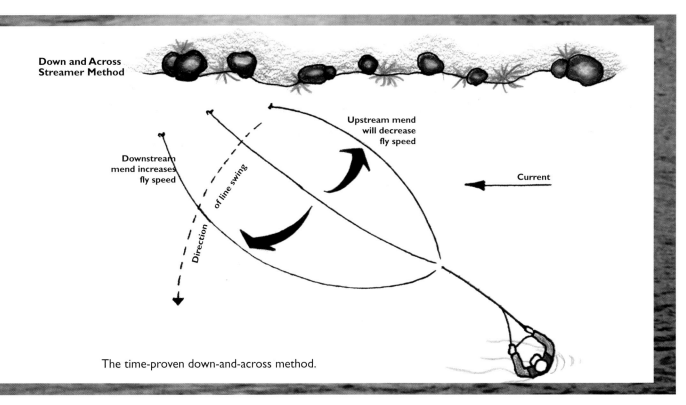

Down and Across Streamer Method

Downstream mend increases fly speed

Direction of line swing

Upstream mend will decrease fly speed

Current

The time-proven down-and-across method.

A group of Atlantic salmon and sea trout fishermen from London opened up a whole new world to me in regards to this presentation (and very fine single malt scotch, I might add). The aforementioned style was the only way I had ever treated the drift. While fishing with them it quickly became apparent there were other moves to be made. The downstream mend is a very valuable asset to this technique and will also produce an amazing number of browns on the right day.

For the downstream mend just reverse the directions for the upstream mend. Granted, this sounds overly simple but downstream mending works the opposite way with the opposite effects. It increases the speed with which the

Soft-Loop

← 12" to 14" Loop

This is how the line should be held when fishing down and across.

streamer crosses the pool. Don't expect me to tell you why fly speed makes such a difference, but it does.

You can adjust how fast the swing occurs by how far you mend the line toward the inside downstream bank. My experience has been that downstream mending tends to produce more rainbows than browns unless it is an overcast day. Brown trout seem to be more confident (or secure) to chase streamers in the middle of pools when the day is drizzly and dark. Otherwise they are found nestled under a bank. I know this technique sounds esoteric, and in all honesty it is little used, but when it produces there is nothing else like it.

Curve Cast

It seems no fly fishing "how-to" book is complete without the seemingly obligatory description of the curve cast. The only problem with this is that not only am I personally incapable of performing this cast (and yes I've spent hours trying) I have never once, in all my years of experience, actually seen this cast executed. A few people make cast mends, described in the last chapter, and call them curve casts, but this is as close as I've come. This lack of observance not only applies to the river, but to all the fancy sport shows with their casting ponds as well. Given my skill is obviously lacking in this area, I'll have to refer you elsewhere.

Captain T.L. Edwards and E. Horsfall Turner, two great British casters, address this phenomenon in their wonderful book *The Angler's Cast*. In reference to the curve cast, they write: "The 'Curve Casts-Positive and Negative' occupy a good deal of American newsprint. Many writers have explained, with a wealth of detailed instruction, how to

A nice sized brown which fell to a Muddler Minnow fished down and across.

put a curve in the cast fly line. These curves have been anything from a gradual over-all curve, from rod tip to fly, to neat L-shaped near-right-angle curves-shown by careful diagrams—but never pictures—which whip the point 3ft. of leader round an inconvenient diagrammatic bush, to place the fly over an inconsiderate diagrammatic fish...." They end the dissertation with, "If a cast is not reliable, we fail to see its utility." Truer words were never written. As the saying goes..."I'm from Missouri on this one folks..."

Hooking, Playing and Landing Large Browns

You are probably more than likely to encounter a large brown hooked on the end of a streamer than almost any other fly type so it's only fitting playing and landing large browns is addressed in this chapter.

It is truly amazing the number of things that can go wrong while you are playing a large brown trout. I mean, let's face it, you should always be able to find a few, but the honest big fish only comes along three or four times a season, and this is if you fish a lot. Why not do everything in your power to avoid mistakes when this miraculous event does occur? When talking about big browns I refer to the "Standard Western Unit of Fish Measurement", the brown has to be or should be damn close to, 20 inches in length. As a side note, if you ever want to talk about one of the rare ones you have landed, you better have a photograph or a witness. If either of these are absent you are

better off keeping your mouth shut. Otherwise you will quickly be labeled as an occasional "hacker" at best.

One of the first, and most often overlooked, things you should do is check and sharpen your hook regularly. Failing to do this is sloppily inefficient, and ultimately provides a false economy. Streamers are heavy flies by nature, and regardless of how good a caster you think you are, one sloppy backcast and your hook point can disappear. Keeping your hook sharp is one of the more ignored aspects of fly fishing. Ironically it is also one of the sport's easier things to do successfully. The new ceramic hook hones do a great job, and virtually never wear out. In this case, better fishing through technology; purchase one and use it.

OK, you haven't dinged your hook point on a rock and it is sharp. The big brown you've been fishing over all season finally grabs a streamer retrieved parallel to the bank. Set the hook! Thousands of nice browns are lost every year, (sadly about the same number are blamed on barbless hooks) simply because the angler failed to concentrate after the initial grab. One of the best ways to set the hook is to give the line a couple of quick, light tugs with the hand you were stripping in line with. Don't overdo it, but pull hard enough to sink the hook to its deepest part.

Something should probably be said here about the fish-holding capabilities of barbed versus barbless hooks. For brown trout fishing, after rather lengthy observations, I'm a big advocate of barbless hooks. For years, I've listened to clients blame barbless hooks (instead of lack of ability and practice) for lost fish. The reality of the matter is simply this: of the thousand or so browns I've been fortunate enough to either catch myself or assist clients in landing, almost without exception, the hook, regardless of barb condition, has always been a) buried to the bend of the hook and b) hooked in the corner of the brown's jaw. Barbless hooks achieve the same penetration (if not more because there is no barb to pro-

Always hold a rod as close to the reel as possible when playing a fish.

vide resistance) and have the same holding power as barbed hooks. Second, if a brown is poorly hooked chances are you won't be able to keep him on, with or without a barb. Browns hooked in the roof of the mouth are notorious for this. This usually occurs when a brown takes the fly by coming up on it from directly downstream. I've witnessed sea trout hooked in the roof of the mouth with #6 treble hooks (barbed) get off. The bottom line in this barbed versus barbless business is barbless hooks are easier to remove from the brown after you've landed it. It makes the whole process easier on the fish, and as fly fishermen continue to grow in numbers I feel we owe it to the resource.

The third rule of playing a large brown trout is to let the fish take line. Assuming you have the proper drag setting on your reel, and the fish is in open water, let 'er rip. All too often anglers "seize up" and grab the line tight only to break the fish off. Trust your reel. Reels are unemotional

Dale Sexton releases a female brown.

acid to be produced. While in people this only causes soreness, for a brown trout this can mean death.

One last thing to watch when attempting to land a large brown is shallow water. Never try to bring a large brown to hand in water shallower than knee deep. A brown will feel the stream bottom and start to thrash around. One of the first things to happen is the fish will gain a purchase with its tail and quickly push upward, causing slack to enter your line and the hook to drop out. Another reason to avoid this is because while flopping on the gravel the brown might scrape scales off making it susceptible to disease.

If you have one handy, a net might be a good thing to use to hold the fish while you remove your fly. Whether to use a net or not is really an individual choice. I haven't yet been able to make up my mind. I've used one enough to create a few prejudices, but not enough to wholeheartedly endorse them. If you are going to use one make sure it has a soft nylon mesh net-bag. Some of the early nets had bags made of knotted hard nylon. These were terribly hard on fish. Also if you are the kind of angler who is going to squeeze the fish to death once it's in the net, leave the net at home. The best way to release a large brown is to simply reach down, grab your hook at the bend and slide it out.

Dale Sexton holds a male brown.

inanimate objects that don't get excited or use poor judgment. While the big brown is taking line directly from the reel you can certainly help out, but do so with the rod.

Besides for casting, fly rods are designed to be long and flexible for another reason. Holding the rod as close to the reel as possible will allow you to put tremendous pressure on the fish without breaking the tippet. Also get in the habit of playing these big browns by holding the rod parallel to the water's surface. The saltwater guides call this technique "down and dirty."

Another helpful hint is to apply pressure in the opposite direction you want the fish to swim. For example, if you are trying to keep a hooked brown from reaching a shallow downstream riffle get below him and apply downstream tension. Well over 90 percent of the time this will cause the fish to reverse its fight upstream, away from the riffle. Once you have the fish in the vicinity you want to land him, start changing direction with the fly rod while maintaining constant pressure. This causes the fish to have to change direction quickly, causing a feeling of vertigo and the fish quickly surrenders. This way you can comfortably land the fish before it really starts to exert itself. Brown trout are like humans in that if they strain too much the muscles begin to work anaerobically, causing lactic

There are a few instances when this task can become complicated. Fishing out of a drift boat or on a river with a very heavy current are two that come to mind. In a river with heavy current net your fish and then quickly move to a back-water area to revive and release it. When angling out of a drift boat, net the fish and bend over the side of the boat to release it. Under no circumstances should you bring the brown trout inside the boat. I can guarantee a fish brought into the boat will end up flopping around on the floor of the boat. Sometime during the process, before the photo, after the photo, while removing the hook, etc., eventually that trout will end up flopping around on the floor of the boat, and will then be dead.

This is a rather lengthy dissertation on one man's streamer fishing prejudice. Use common sense and try to protect the resource, and both you and the brown trout will be rewarded.

CHAPTER SIX

DRY FLIES

The Allure

Dry fly fishing for brown trout is as old as any fly fishing there is. One of the earliest written accounts of the sport is from the third century A.D., when an early scribe discusses wool, chicken feathers and hooks in the same paragraph. He then excitedly compares the surface take of a brown trout to an eagle snatching geese off local waters. One of the truly spooky things is how little this has changed.

Recently, during a phone conversation, the editor of a fly fishing magazine brought this to my attention. He works for a company which is in the process of bringing out a new fly tying magazine. He had actually called to tell me he was going to purchase an article I had sent him, but while he was on the phone I quickly seized the opportunity to sell more work.

I started into this great idea for this little-known saltwater pattern: "very easy to tie, and an absolute killer on several different species… All the magazines want saltwater articles, it's the newest fad." Before I could hit full stride (The Desperate Salesman Blues—has the refrain of "just how great it's going to be…") he shut me off. Seems the corporate machine he works for had just completed a little market research; specifically they had conducted two surveys 20 years apart which in the end had arrived at the same conclusion: Fly fishing is still about catching trout on dry flies. While there are more splinter groups than ever before, the core of the sport hasn't changed one bit.

If anything can make fly fishing any more glorious it has to be casting over a rising brown during the evening's last light. It just doesn't get any better. All fly-caught browns are road-markers on an angler's journey, but the ones caught on dries also represent milestones. Dry-fly-caught browns are so pitifully few compared to the hours spent they are always remembered.

Once on the Bighorn River Mike Conley and I hooked and landed matching 20 inchers, only several casts apart, right at dusk. Both fish were feeding on adult mayflies with only their snouts sticking out from under an algae mat next to the bank. Size 16 Blue Winged Olive Compara-Duns deserve most of the credit.

Above my desk is a photo of a 21 inch brown, which not only represents good fortune, but a rare moment of brilliance as well. We were floating the upper Madison and the salmonflies were just starting to crawl up on the banks and overhanging brush. Although adults were yet to be seen fluttering overhead or flopping (as anybody who has ever fished this famous hatch will attest, these insects are large enough to flop) on the surface, in an act of angling defiance I tied on a MacSalmon. Pretty soon I was taking a fair amount of flack from my friend rowing the boat.

"What are you wasting our time for with that damn dry fly?" my friend's voice boomed from the rower's seat behind me, "If you can't see they are obviously on the nymphs I'm going to pull over and you can row while I fish."

There was some sound reasoning behind this as I had not brought a trout to the net in about 45 minutes. Needless to say, about the time I was going to switch back to a Bitch Creek it happened. Two things were amazing about this brown—one was its size, and the second was that it had leapt completely clear of the water and taken the MacSalmon on the way back into the river. Then, as I seem to have a habitual need to do while playing big browns, I choked. Too much pressure was applied and I broke the fish off on its first downstream run. This is very difficult to do while you are floating downstream in a drift boat at the same speed as the current. To shorten the tale I was then wisely removed from the casting position and made to sit and contemplate my mistakes from the rower's seat.

A well-stocked dry fly box is essential during the Montana salmonfly hatch.

And the Moment of Brilliance?

After finally making it back to the front of the boat, I was still "screwing around" with the MacSalmon as we floated the stretch immediately upstream of the take-out, when an even larger brown hit. Miraculously, everything stayed glued together as I played, netted, begged for a photograph and released the trout in front of the boat ramp gallery. Guides I knew called me certain names so loudly it made several of their clients blush. I also remember a higher than usual bar tab that evening as well. Milestones all.

A Brief Look Back

The dry fly as we know it came into being in the early to mid 1800s—debate surrounds whether it happened in the 30s or 50s. Other than this, unlike nymph or streamer history, dry flies have been pretty well documented. The whole dry fly history business, in my opinion and not those who make their living from this sort of thing, seems to read like a bad made-for-TV movie. Early names like Theodatus Garlick and Sylvanus Swangill (admittedly only a pen name) help support this theory. While dry flies are certainly important to the fly angler in search of browns, they will never be his/her bread and butter. So much has been written about this history it would really serve no purpose to replicate it here. If early dry fly history interests you there are several good books devoted to this; a good place to start is Paul Schullery's *American Fly Fishing—*

A History. Vincent Marinaro's *In The Ring Of The Rise* is also a very important book which covers dry fly history.

Knowledge and Organization

Hooking and landing brown trout on dry flies, when the opportunity presents itself, requires the most cerebral energy of any of the tactics described thus far. Many moving parts must be mastered. Probably the most logical place to start is to identify what insect the brown is taking from the surface. There are many ways to go about this. I'll go out on a limb and say at a bare minimum you should be able to recognize the "big ones."

The "big ones" are: caddis, mayflies, stoneflies and midges. Take the time to learn and recognize these as they will always be a staple of the brown trout's diet, regardless of where you are fishing for them. There are many good angling books which describe all of these foods in their entirety.

Aside from the "big ones" a successful dry fly brown trout angler should also have a firm grip on insects of regional importance. This only requires you stumble into a cranefly or spruce moth hatch once without the proper pattern. And obviously no dry fly list is complete without mention of the terrestrials.

It should be noted, a great place to find this information is your state university or the County Extension Service. Somewhere in your area there is a "bug-head" who has put together a photocopy publication of some kind which will prove invaluable for dry fly identification

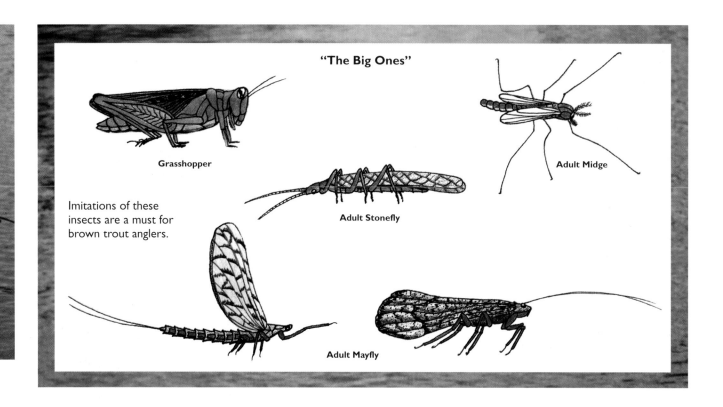

"The Big Ones"

Grasshopper

Adult Midge

Adult Stonefly

Imitations of these insects are a must for brown trout anglers.

Adult Mayfly

and tying ideas. I once called the local Extension Service and asked about grasshopper information—a three-pound box of information showed up the following week. Seems there are over 75 sub-species in Montana alone.

You might feel this is an overly simple issue for an advanced book, but it's not. The number of fly fishermen who are unable to identify a mayfly would astound you. I'm not even talking about an individual species of mayfly, just mayflies in general. This is supported by the number of anglers you see fishing with attractor patterns every year. Attractor patterns are far and away the most popular dry flies sold every year, but browns do not consistently fall for them. The point being, if the fly you use most happens to be a lime green Double Humpy you have some work to do before you should consider yourself a brown trout dry fly fisherman. Before this starts to smack of snobbery, it should be pointed out that by becoming a serious student of dry fly fishing much of the personal satisfaction this particular sport has to offer will be discovered.

Deciding which flies to carry with you to emulate these insects should follow logical steps. The first piece of advice for dry fly selection is: carry as few as you dare, but learn to use what you carry well. If there is any part of the dry fly process I dare say can be simplified it would have to be fly selection. Countless photographs show the nation's dry fly "experts" wearing what look like small suitcases strapped to their chests. A few, who decided this file drawer system wasn't enough, have even added full fly vests to complete their ensemble. While it is not my intention to imply these folks don't catch a lot of trout I merely question the point of diminishing returns. Could it be they might catch the same number carrying half the flies? If the

trout you are pursuing happens to be brown the answer is a hearty "yes."

The insects brown trout are most interested in, with a few minor exceptions, have very similar life cycles. Once these insects end up on the surface as adults there are only three things that matter—size, silhouette and color are the criteria all dry flies should be judged against. I'll even go one step further and say correct presentation will outshine all three of these—but more on this in a minute.

Size

Providing your presentation is decent, fly size, more than any other variable, will determine whether or not that large toothy brown sucking dries from the surface is going to be interested in your offering. By now the first question will be, "you mean to tell me that if a brown trout is feeding on midges I could probably take him on a #18 Elk Hair Caddis?" The answer: "Absolutely!" Why you would want to do this after you have figured out all the necessary information could be questioned, but it can certainly be done on a regular basis.

One of the problems when discussing fly size is that for some reason most fly fishermen seem to equate this with hook size. A certain way to increase your catch (and hopefully release) of browns is to pretend this relationship doesn't exist. Obviously the two aren't mutually exclusive, but just because you are tying a #20 fly doesn't mean it has to be on a #20 hook. As a matter of fact I don't recommend tying a fly on anything smaller than a #18, and I'm damn picky about the hooks used to do this. The simple truth: Hooks smaller than #18 are incapable of regularly holding large browns or browns hooked in heavy current. No doubt it occasionally happens, but if the browns don't care what size hook the fly is tied on, why risk it?

Admittedly this method has its limits but they are broader than you would expect. Obviously, you will probably not have much success tying Griffith's Gnats on a #1/0 salmon hook. A general rule of thumb for this is you can safely "cheat" by at least two hook sizes, and some of the time by three, if short-shanked hooks are involved. You can feel confident in tying your #18 midge pattern on a #14 hook, and possibly even a #12 if the hook is a 1X short.

This not only increases the amount of gape available for secure hook-ups, but the hook's bend and eye will be strong enough to hold. And best of all it certainly doesn't matter to the browns!

Silhouette

The reason I used the Griffith's Gnat and Elk Hair Caddis comparison, aside from the fact I used to make this substitution routinely, is because if viewed from below the two flies have similar silhouettes.

After size, silhouette has to be one of the major distinguishing characteristics brown trout key on while deciding whether or not to take. This observation is in contradiction to what some other folks have written. This observation is based on very little scientific fact but rather on countless hours of fishing for browns. Most surface feeding activity occurs on long flat stretches of river. Unless it is a very profuse caddis hatch you will seldom find browns actively feeding on dries in runs or riffles. As a result browns take full advantage of this slower moving water to inspect a dry fly while rising to it.

Danny Johnson about ready to release a brown taken with a size 10 MacHopper.

Small Fly on a Large Hook

Elk Hair Caddis

A small fly tied on a large hook. This technique is especially suited to parachute patterns.

While fishing this type of water, most people claim exacting imitations are the rule but I feel most are more trouble than they are worth. Here's why: The flat water/exacting imitation school tends to go overboard needlessly when it comes to dry fly design. When I talk about silhouettes I am referring to them from the fish's point of view. The fish only sees the bottom two-thirds of the fly! There is no reason for this line of thinking to extend above the surface of the water. For years tiers and fly designers have created these absolutely perfect flies; beautiful to look at, a pleasure to own, but absolutely miserable to locate once cast further than five feet. It quickly becomes apparent many fly designers fish fewer hours than claimed.

The perfect dry fly should be an exact imitation on the bottom two-thirds of the fly and the upper one-third should be designed for the angler. By this I mean the fly should be uncluttered and as visible as possible to the angler. This holds especially true on flat water during low light conditions.

J.M. Conley is the angler who has influenced my thinking about this more than any other. He was the first person I ever saw to tie almost all his flies with either a post wing or a fluorescent overwing (if the fly recipe called for a tent-wing). Two good examples of this are the fly patterns mentioned earlier. Conley ties his Griffith's Gnat with a post-wing sticking straight up out of the fly's body. To ensure it lands properly every time he slightly trims the underside of the grizzly hackle flush with the point of the hook. The fly does not have any choice other than to land right side up every time. His Elk Hair Caddis are tied with a bright overwing allowing the angler to quickly locate them regardless of how far they are tossed. Once again, the underside of these flies are exact imitations and are all the brown trout sees; blindingly bright colors on top of the fly make no difference whatsoever to the brown trout.

Griffith's Gnat tied with a
black post-wing for visibility.

Color and shades of light vary tremendously depending on the time of day or the cast of sky. To a lesser extent this probably even varies region to region. Keeping this in mind, the two best colors to start with are black and fluorescent orange. While fishing smooth water on a bright day, a fluorescent orange post-wing, only several millimeters tall, will stick out like an 18 foot inflatable raft. Fishing in low (flat) light created by either sunset or sunrise is greatly enhanced by using a solid black wing material. Try both of these colors to start with and don't be afraid to experiment as local conditions allow.

Fly Color

Fly color, while it takes somewhat of a back seat to the two previously mentioned aspects of dry fly criteria, is not something to be completely ignored. A common mistake many brown trout anglers make, when it comes to color, is they attempt to substitute their judgment for the trout's. This results in a dry fly that is either completely the wrong color or one that comes close, but its development stopped before it was improved.

First rule of dry fly color: "A dry fly can never reach perfection." Regardless of how many fish the fly has taken never start thinking you can't make it better. Fly colors arrived at by this method tend to be non-traditional but highly effective. Many times the color will not even match (to your eyes) the natural you are trying to imitate. How the brown trout sees this fly is a different story completely.

After awhile it almost becomes easy to judge an effective dry fly by this method. When somebody pulls out their "hot new pattern" and it is an exact replication of the natural, be cautious. If, on the other hand, the fly color appears off or is different than any natural you have ever seen, think about going home and tying a dozen.

So far this has all been pretty theoretical. Since this is supposed to be a "how to" book some practical information about dry fly color might be prudent. For the following advice on colors I went no further than my own fly

vest. These colors have been tried and proven over a great many trips to the river, and yes they are still in development!

As I look around in my caddis box I see the most common color for dry fly dubbing is an unsightly greenish-cream combination with a small hint of orange. Picture a bowl of split-pea soup with a cup or two of milk suddenly poured in. I'm not even sure how to describe the hint of orange. This is the weirdest color. Most of the others are standard colors: brown, tan, light green, black and red.

Most of my mayfly patterns are either an off cream-mustard combination or they are a darkish brown-green. In the corner of this box are some that are almost white in color. About one evening a year, usually in August, in southwestern Montana you can plan on finding browns feeding on solid white mayflies. I'm pitifully ignorant of this subspecies, but have caught enough browns on them to know they are not to be ignored. For some reason the darkish brown-green dubbing is a mixture that seems to take different ingredients every year to achieve the same color combination. The end result should almost be more brown than green and when dubbed on the hook should resemble the standard military camouflage.

My Trico (*Tricorythodes*) box has mostly spent-wing dries tied in black or light gray. Another observation of relevance is the color of the wing material on all of my Trico's. All the old flies have wings constructed of a material that almost glows, it's so fluorescent white. These caught fish only occasionally and, thus, why they are still in the box. The newer, and more productive, ones have their wings made with the same material, but the color is a light tan and not nearly as bright. The unfortunate thing is I can't remember if this was one of those few great revelations a fly fisherman occasionally has or if somebody taught me this trick. Either way, the bottom line is, a more subtle color on Trico wings will catch more browns.

Terrestrials

When brown trout are on terrestrials nothing else is an adequate substitute. Grasshopper season comes immediately to mind. During grasshopper season large browns, normally the wariest of all the trouts, start to act downright goofy. A brown trout chasing grasshoppers will make a rut-crazed mule deer look intelligent.

They become so aggressive it becomes almost comical. An example of this, forever etched in my mind, occurred while I was guiding a lady on her first outing with a fly rod. We were fishing a large creek in the prime of grasshopper season. She had just started to get the hang of the cast and the retrieve. Her fourth cast was poorly executed and caused her grasshopper to land clumsily on the shallow side of the creek. Suddenly a 15 inch brown trout exploded from the deep end of the stream and in three large greyhound jumps across the stream, smashed the fly and took off upstream. Unfortunately, somewhere around the brown's second jump the lady lost her composure and simultaneously screamed and threw the fly

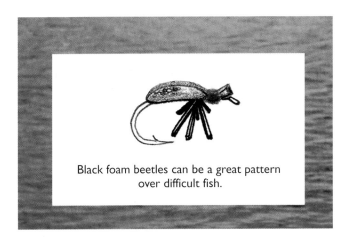

Black foam beetles can be a great pattern over difficult fish.

rod into the water in front of her, "What was that?" she shrieked.

Somewhat dumbfounded by the fish and my client's actions, "a brown trout," was the only answer I could muster as I attempted to retrieve the fly rod and reel from the creek.

Another great terrestrial pattern, which remains largely overlooked, is the beetle. When I say it is a great pattern, I don't mean as a searching pattern but rather a great one for difficult fish. If you happen to be working over a brown that has refused several different pattern offerings try a beetle. Beetle patterns tied with the closed-cell foam seem to work best. I don't know why, but even if the brown trout is working on caddis or small *Baetis* mayflies the old foam beetle is just unusual enough to cause the fish to momentarily drop its guard.

My biggest complaint with most of the current terrestrial patterns in use is not silhouette or size, but color. The odd thing about this is terrestrials are the easiest to collect and examine. Without a long dissertation on terrestrial colors, the patterns with soft neutral browns, greens and yellows are going to serve you best. I don't know who originally had the idea of putting red into a grasshopper pattern.

Fly Equipment For Dries

Rods

Here is where things become fun. The fly rod was basically designed to be used for casting dry flies. Rods for streamer and nymph angling are just now starting to come into their own. As you can tell from reading the previous two chapters I'm a big advocate of stiff actioned graphite rods for most of my fishing. Casting a dry fly, however, remains the exception.

If you want the opportunity to truly enjoy the action of a split bamboo rod, dry fly fishing is the way to do it. Cane rods have a very soft, methodical action. Some folks even get misty-eyed and proclaim using them next to "magical." I guess I'm a little too practical for this line of thought, but they do have a great many attributes. Being of a slower action, cane rods naturally cause you to be a little more accurate with your casting. You will also dis-

cover you break off fewer fish on the initial strike with cane rods. And, aside from both these features, cane rods can be just plain fun to fool around with. Of course the "down side" to split bamboo rods is they can be a maintenance nightmare. If your cane rod doesn't worry you while you are fishing with it then you are probably doing something wrong.

Another, often overlooked, rod material for dry fly rods is fiberglass. "The Golden Age of Glass" happened in the 1960s and the early 1970s. Quality rods by R.L. Winston, Russ Peak and others are still available on the used market. These fiberglass rods have excellent tapers and actions for dry fly fishing, but are often overlooked for graphite rods of a far lesser quality because "...everybody knows graphite is the modern rod material of choice." Another nice attribute of this is glass rods can usually be purchased for a song from used tackle dealers. If you get the opportunity give one a try, they are a delight to toss a dry fly with.

If your dry fly rod is to be graphite, make sure it has an internal-spigot type ferrule. More delicate than the sleeve type ferrule, an internal-spigot makes for a more sensitive rod on forward casts.

Since most of the time good dry fly presentations are a close range affair, I'll even soften on rod length for a dry fly rod. While there is no sense to owning a rod under nine feet in length for nymph or streamer fishing, the best length for a surface rod is 8'6". This length will allow for soft-actioned casting while wade fishing, but is short enough to provide snappy deliveries when fishing pocket water from a moving drift boat.

Handles on dry fly rods should be shorter and more compact than on rods for other uses. Cigar shaped handles are best. This forces the same position of the casting hand on the rod grip time after time, which breeds muscle memory, and in turn consistency and accuracy.

Line weights for dry fly rods are an individual thing. With two major exceptions, whatever line weight you fish best with is what you should use. The first exception is the line weight of your choice should be capable of quickly and efficiently landing a brown trout in a safe manner. By safe manner I mean an elapsed time from hook-up to release which will allow a fish to swim away with the greatest likelihood of survival. It hasn't been so bad in the last few years but the "in" thing used to be to see how large a trout you could land on the lightest tackle. This started with fun intentions but soon got carried away. The anglers featured in the advertisements, and who also wrote the articles, had the ability to land large fish unharmed in a short amount of time with the small line weights. Unfortunately, the majority of fly fishermen don't fish one-quarter of the time these folks do and have one-sixteenth of their talent. This resulted in many dead trout when they were released.

The second exception is the currently fashionable trend of "overloading" the rod. This usually entails someone putting, say, a seven weight line on a rod clearly

A cane rod can be a wonderful dry fly rod for small streams.

attractive. If you absolutely can't live without one on one of your lighter dry fly rods, make sure the barrel of the seat is made of hardwood. Maple, if available, is a good choice for both aesthetics and durability. Wood barrels will not get soft like those made of cork.

Reels

A valuable secret for purchasing a reel for your dry fly rod, like with your streamer reel, is to buy one designed for the next larger line size. While reel capacity for dry fly fishing is not very critical, the condition of your fly line is. The smaller the amount of backing you wind your floating line around the higher the chance of the line being pigtailed when it is pulled from the reel. A larger diameter reel will allow the line to remain in larger, looser coils.

Another important thing to look for in a dry fly reel is a good smooth drag. Spend some time checking this out. Some of the cheaper disc drag reels jerk more than the good ones with a pawl-click drag system.

If it is possible to find the model reel you would like to purchase with backing and fly line on it so much the better. Set the drag on a setting in the middle of the available range and grab hold of the fly line, letting the reel dangle. Does the reel inch smoothly toward the floor? If not, keep loosening the setting until it does. Watch how smoothly it does this. If the reel seems to get stuck between two drag settings, one where it won't move and the other where it almost free spools toward the floor, keep looking for a new reel. Ideally the reel should smoothly lower itself to the floor at the same speed regardless of how much line is removed from the spool.

marked for a six, and the whole concept is utter nonsense. All rods are engineered and designed to perform with the line weight printed on the rod. Changing rod performance by altering line weights truly says: "I don't care for the action of this rod as it was designed so I'm going to slow it down by putting more of a strain on it." Instead, spend more time looking around for the rod design and action you really want.

The best all-around line weight for dry fly rods is probably a five. This is small enough for delicate presentations, handling fine tippets and making smaller trout the fun they really are. On the other hand, a five weight still has the backbone to land the occasional gnarly, gap-toothed brown you only encounter once or twice a season.

The only other part of a dry fly rod I have strong feelings about is the reel seat. Regardless of what the manufacturer or the fly shop salesman tells you, don't purchase a rod with a slide-band reel seat. I have yet to see one which held the reel securely on the rod, especially after some use. Unfortunately this type of reel seat is the most

Leaders

Dry fly leaders, like dry flies, should never be viewed in any way that judges them perfect. Oh, you can use a recipe for many years which works well, but don't ever think there isn't a better performing leader.

One of the basic principles of dry fly leaders is to keep it very simple. People spend far too much time worrying about arcane leader recipes when a simple design will turn over in 90 percent of all situations—I'll even go so far as to say 95 percent of all situations. Leader design and application used to change between flies. Leaders approaching 20 feet in length were reserved for small midges and Tricos. Dry fly leaders under six feet in length were mandatory for fishing bushy

10-Foot Dry Fly Leader								
Fly Line / Distance	2.5 Feet	1 Foot	1 Foot	1.5 Feet	.5 Foot	.5 Foot	.5 Foot	2.5 Feet
Breaking Strength	25.7 lbs.	23.1 lbs.	16.7 lbs.	12.8 lbs.	8.6 lbs.	6.8 lbs.	5.5 lbs.	4.6 lbs.
Diameter Metric & Conventional	.40 mm	.35 mm	.30 mm	.25 mm (0X equiv.)	.20 mm (4X equiv.)	.18 mm (3X equiv.)	.16 mm (4X equiv.)	.14 mm (5X equiv.)

A recipe for a functional 10-foot-long dry fly leader.

Elk Hair Caddis' in the choppy riffles during the middle of a hatch. Oddly enough if you spend more time with presentation and technique, exotic dry fly leader recipes become less important.

Most of my leaders are about 10 feet in length and tippet sizes never go below 6X. Leaders should have smooth transitional tapers. Occasionally the knots might need to be coated with clear fingernail polish or glue if you are fishing in water with a lot of algae. For all brown trout fishing the leader should be attached to your fly line with a nail knot. This knot has been used to land thousands of browns, and when properly tied is fail proof. For tying your own leaders use the double surgeon's knot. It is not only stronger than the blood knot, but is also easier to tie in low light conditions.

Once you find or adopt a recipe tie up a bunch in advance. Time spent on the stream should be spent with your fly in the water, not tying leaders. As long as you store them somewhere dark they will remain in good condition for several seasons. The leader recipes included here represent trial and error more than innovative thought. Give them a try, tweak them to your liking, and above all keep trying new variations until you have the utmost confidence in your particular design.

Techniques

Presentation, Presentation, Presentation!

A whole drift boat full of the world's finest tackle will not catch brown trout without proper presentation of the dry fly. Conversely, the cheapest fly rod and reel outfit can be used to catch plenty of browns if the angler can recognize proper presentation. Proper fly presentation is critical, and is best learned in a series of steps. One of the great things about a river or stream is that it has water configurations for everyone. These different water types can be learned, but the whole is best mastered by conquering the parts. However, discipline is required to do this.

The first step is to assess your ability. Be brutally honest with yourself as to how effectively you can fish a dry fly. Do you still put fish "down", or finally get the fly to where you think the fish should have taken, only to have it keep drifting?

Upstream Presentation

The second step is for one entire season to always fish your dries upstream. Hear me out before you start to moan. If you want to become a deadly dry fly fisherman take one entire season and only cast to areas from below them. This is not to say dries should not be fished across the current, in fact, they can be very effective this way, but one thing at a time.

More than any other aspect of fly fishing for brown trout, dry fly fishing is centered around muscle memory. Tennis and golf are very similar in this respect. By always presenting a fly from downstream of the fish you are going to become intimately familiar with all the different currents, line control options and techniques unique to this position. Mistakes made in judging distance will not be as critical from directly downstream. Your innate ability to present the fly from this position will not only increase tenfold, but will become ingrained so deeply you will no longer have to consciously think about what you are doing. Occasionally you'll hear a top-notch angler describe an angling experience as being in "the zone". This is the state of mind/ability he is talking about. Believe it or not you will catch more browns on dries during this season than any season before. Another incidental benefit of doing this (if you honestly do it) is it will also make you a better wader. You have to think more to always put yourself in a downstream position.

Cross Stream—Single Current

The next season take on another new type of water. Look for single cross-current opportunities. The ideal situation is to find a brown feeding on the surface in a spot where only one current speed exists between you and the trout. Avoid areas where different current speeds need to be cast across simultaneously. For the remainder of this season limit yourself to dry fly fishing only to trout in either this position or to those approachable from downstream. This will allow you to perfect upstream and downstream presentation and mending. Once again concentrate on how different current speeds effect the movement of your fly line. Focusing on these individual current speeds, one at a time, will teach you the most difficult aspects of suc-

A brown trout which fell prey to a black foam beetle.

BROWN TROUT FLY FISHING: A PRACTICAL GUIDE

cessfully fishing a dry fly—line control. This is what separates memorable brown trout anglers from the OK, and the OK from the hopeless.

When casting across a single current, aside from your cast placement, the most important decision you face is whether to make an upstream or downstream mend. For the record, my first choice is always the upstream mend. Mending upstream will usually leave you the opportunity to make another mend without putting additional line out on the water. Actually, as the common cross-current cast floats downstream it allows you to pick up some line. The less line you have out the quicker you are going to set the hook after a strike. So when would you use a downstream mend? One of the best times is when fishing around structure that, for whatever reason, can't be covered drag-free by an upstream presentation or mend. One of the big secrets of a successful downstream mend is to allow for an extra 10-12 feet of line in your initial cast. A downstream mend tends to diminish cast length quicker than an upstream one. Mending with the current appears to be the most logical reason for this. In theory this shouldn't happen, but it does so be sure to compensate for it. Another great time to use a downstream mend is when fishing from a moving drift boat. If the person on the oars is paying attention he/she will hold the boat speed just barely below that of the current. A downstream mend allows your fly to drift the same speed as the current, and will require less rod work than using the upstream mend.

Cross-Stream—Multiple Currents

This is the most demanding and frustrating of all dry fly fishing presentations. Frustration lies with multiple current speeds simply because it is virtually impossible to consistently fish them correctly. Oh, you'll do OK most of the time, but the big brown finning around in the back eddy sipping small mayflies, several current speeds away will embarrass you more times than not. Anyone who tells you they can keep the dry fly from dragging in these situations is a liar.

The easiest "quick fix" for this dilemma is to remove as much distance as possible between you and the area you wish to cover. It is very common to see inexperienced anglers standing three or four current speeds away, attempting to cast to a rising fish in a tough area like this. Unfortunately, the water they are standing in is only knee deep. As long as they don't spook the fish, there is no reason they couldn't position themselves just 10 feet directly downstream from the rising brown. Doing this will allow a cleaner presentation with less line or if the angler is really sneaky you can sometimes get close enough so that you only need your leader on the water. So before you try any of the fancy casts (which seem to be all the rage in the new instructional videos), simply try to eliminate the need for them first. Captain T.L. Edwards and E. Horsfall Turner summed up this approach in their book *The Angler's Cast* when they wrote, "The quality of a cast is the measure of its capacity to catch fish."

Now, let's assume there is still three or four different current speeds between you and a large brown, and the water between is deep beyond approach. The first cast that is usually taught for this situation is the S or "wiggle" cast. This is performed by shaking the fly rod horizontally, before the line hits the water on the forward cast. While this cast works great for streamers and nymphs, it has some inherent problems preventing it from being a consistent producer in this dry fly situation. First there is no real way to coordinate how many bends or "S"s you'll get in the line, and secondly it is impossible to put the bends in the fly line at the correct sizes and intervals to actually prevent drag. The best way to accomplish a drag-free float under these conditions is to make an upstream mend during your final cast and then quickly follow this through with more mends once you see how the different current speeds are going to treat your fly line. Obviously, faster speeds require immediate mending, while some of the slower speeds may never require any mending. Addressing multiple current speeds in this fashion will prevent one of the "S"s or bends from landing downstream in the faster current and immediately dragging your fly past the fish. This method requires quite a bit of practice. Making two or three fast accurate mends without moving the fly will be maddening initially, and regardless of how good you get you are still going to make mistakes and experience missed opportunities. Stick with it and remember by the time the season rolls around you are working on this technique you will already have two other dry fly techniques in your arsenal of tricks.

By the way, every so often you'll encounter a rising brown trout in a spot you can't present a drag free fly to. Tip your hat and move on—these are the browns your memory will carry longer than any other.

In the end, once all the evidence is assembled, with the possible exception of an upstream presentation on smooth water, there isn't a single ideal dry fly cast, but rather a combination of many. Every dry fly angler will have to kill snakes in their own way, these experiences are offered for whatever they may be worth!

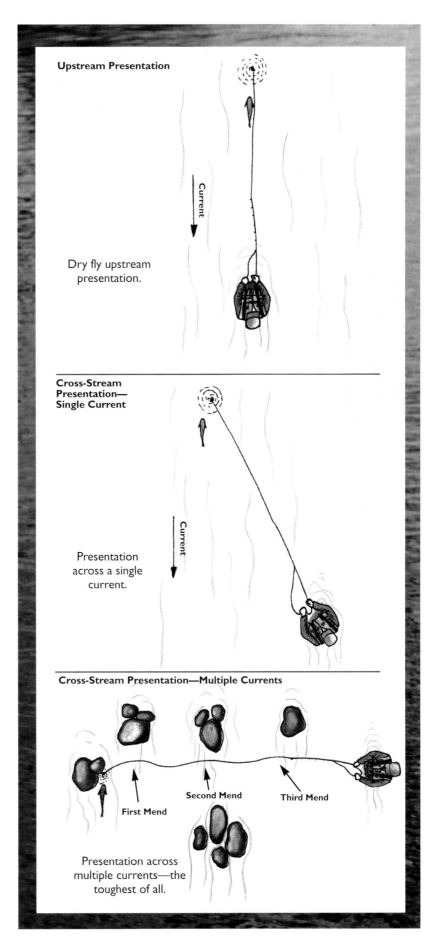

Upstream Presentation

Current

Dry fly upstream presentation.

Cross-Stream Presentation— Single Current

Current

Presentation across a single current.

Cross-Stream Presentation—Multiple Currents

First Mend

Second Mend

Third Mend

Presentation across multiple currents—the toughest of all.

CHAPTER SEVEN

NIGHT MOVES

Secrecy

Night fishing for brown trout is one of those techniques you don't hear much about. There appear to be several reasons for this. Not many anglers actually do it with any great regularity in the first place, and of those who have tried it there seem to be two types. The first type are those who have actually tried it, and as a result, have some very embarrassing story which "they would rather not go into". Stories I have heard involve beavers, muskrats and bears, up to a few which actually involved a near death experience. These anglers are not going to try night fishing again any time soon. This leaves the second type of night angler—those who have tried it and are so damn successful they're not going to discuss all the details with you. Not that they are rude necessarily, it's just that they are more interested in results than reflection. Believe me, this kind is the minority, but they are out there. These people are the ones you want to discover.

Origins

Night fishing for brown trout really got its start in England and Ireland. Both of these areas have a rich tradition in angling for sea trout after the sun goes down. These traditions continue today and sometimes border on the religious. Recently I received a call from a friend of mine who lives southwest of London. He was in the process of putting together a trip for sea-run browns to South America. Why? Well, travelling half way around the world to stand chest deep in frigid water at night to cast for large browns is his idea of a good time. Come to think of it it's mine too, and that was one of the reasons he called in the first place (it was great to hear all the details, but in the end financial constraints prevented me from making the trip). This is precisely the way serious brown trout angling is handled in these countries—it's not one technique among many, it's simply the way it's done!

This is partly due, I'm sure, to the fact most Europeans feel both brown trout (and sea trout) and Atlantic salmon feed more actively during low light conditions. I've fished for all of the aforementioned species during both daylight and nighttime hours and experience has shown me several things of interest. Sea trout are definitely more on the feed after dark, while brown trout can be caught anytime. The caveat to this is you are more likely to catch larger browns at night than you will during the day. Atlantic salmon feed whenever they feel like it, and it will always be when your line is not in the water!

Domestic Darkness

In this nation fishing for browns at night really got rolling in the East specifically in Pennsylvania. One of the first fly fishermen to popularize night fishing in this and other areas was George Harvey. Mr. Harvey has had a long and distinguished career. He was the person responsible for creating organizing and starting the now famous fly fishing courses at Penn State University in 1934. I doubt anyone has taught more people to fly fish. But, aside from this, one of his even greater achievements (in my opinion) was the development of a series of what he calls "pusher" type night flies. So named because of the way they are tied so as to create a wake when they are retrieved. It was a Harvey "pusher" fly which has been responsible for many large nighttime browns being taken, including the Pennsylvania state record, a 15 pound, 5 ounce brown which was taken by his teaching replacement at Penn State, Joe Humphries. I'd say this qualifies the pattern. More on the presentation of this pattern later. While I've never net Mr. Harvey I have been fortunate enough to guide President Carter several times and he speaks about George Harvey with reverence.

It also should not go unnoticed that Pennsylvania has produced another gentleman who also helped popular-

DALE SEXTON

An outstanding brown.

ize night fishing. Jim Bashline has written an excellent book about the subject entitled N*ight Fishing For Trout; The Final Frontier*. I recommend it.

If you get serious enough, long enough, you will be taking browns regularly during the daylight hours, and if you are like me eventually pure naked greed will enter the picture. You probably won't notice it at first but eventually you will stay and fish for too long and you will find yourself night fishing. Likely, this first outing will yield some browns, but it will probably also be wrought with complications and frustration because of lack of planning.

In my case this happened on a river we were floating. As complicated and unnerving as it was, only one person could still row the drift boat. This left me free to sit in the bow and fish (and watch and listen for major rocks). As luck would have it we had just finished or so I thought, an excellent last hour of the day with a tremendous caddis hatch. We glided silently down the river while listening to the browns still actively gobbling up the caddis. At the suggestion of my friend rowing the boat, I tied on a #10 Partridge and Peacock soft-hackle. Aside from the fact the browns couldn't leave it alone the first thing I noticed was how quickly a drastic change in hook size became irrelevant. Before dark we had been taking fish on #14s and frankly probably should have been using #16s. After dark, hook size was not only less important I think the larger fly helped the browns locate it easier. I'll cover more on this particular technique later, but first let's look at how to get started.

Preparation

To start with I'm not going to advocate floating rivers at night. The previously mentioned experience occurred on a river both of us were intimately familiar with and it still caused some problems. I'm not predicting gloom, doom or that you can't do it. Just be aware there is an extremely steep learning curve associated with this method.

A far more sane way to start out is by wading. Pick your spots during the day. Areas to look for usually have deep water in close proximity to a shallow riffle. The deep water does not have to be terribly large, only a few deep slots among a riffle may be sufficient. Browns use these slots as travel corridors, working up into these areas while it is still light out, as darkness approaches they eventually work their way out onto the shallow bench. Identify the slots first, my experience has proven that two likely places to look for slots are along the bank and in the middle of riffles that are about knee deep. Obviously every area is different so keep an eye out while you visit these places during daylight hours because at dark all water quickly becomes homogeneous. A good rule to remember is, when looking for a good area, the warmer it is the farther out browns will travel after nightfall and it is more likely they will be in shallower water. Generally, another trend on high traffic water will be for the browns to move from deeper slower water to the riffles. When they aren't bothered, browns will even move from the riffles to the upper elevations of the slower pools. But as they say, "check your local listings".

Fishing an area during the day prior to a night excursion will also help put you ahead. Concentrate on the distance and drift of each cast. Focus on how the fly line moves through the water. Are there any drifts which require special mends? Watch for reverse current areas adjacent to the streambank. While brown trout will not be able to see you, if you take a bad step and muddy water carries upstream ahead of you, your presence will be known very early. Pay extra attention to anything in the way of your backcast, and where in the area you can or can't wade. If available, use any natural or man-made casing platforms you can. They can be anything from a stump to an old bridge piling—anything to keep your backcast in the clear. Make special notes about the landscape. Is the upstream run best cast to while standing just to the left or right of a log or particular stick? All of these things become paramount when it's dark. Don't worry about fishing your night spot the day of the same evening you wish to fish, as long as the area has several hours to rest before it gets dark you'll be fine. It will most likely be a different group of browns using the area at this time anyway.

Even though you want to rest an area several hours before you fish it, always show up at least an hour before nightfall. Without casting a line, watch the spot go dark. Pay particular attention to which individual spots go dark before the others. Reasons for this difference will vary from overhanging cover to the way a particular cloud formation settles in for the night. This will very seldom be a constant. When you are ready to start casting, fish these spots first.

Most all of my night fishing has been on small tributary streams during the peak of the hot summer months. During these months many of the larger, shallower western rivers have temperatures too high for browns to live in comfortably. If they can gain access to the cooler environs of the smaller-tributary, higher-elevation streams they will. After finding these streams a brown will usually only feed sporadically during the day, but will really turn-on after dark.

While a good spot is important don't get so carried away that you forget about access. Simply, how do you plan on getting there? In the East where night fishing started I'm told you can walk to almost anywhere you wish to fish. Things in the West are a little different. Here a particular pool might require two day-time float trips followed

A very colorful brown.

by some night fishing and having to spending the night. You are not as likely to walk in and walk out, so plan ahead.

All around, familiarity and preparation will help in several ways. Most importantly it will make you more efficient at covering the water, which will ultimately lead to more fish. Also, familiarity will help in an unexpected way. Fishing at night tends to be a little unnerving. This is both part of the fun as well as part of the problem. Being comfortable in an area will calm anxieties enabling you to enjoy it more, and help to prevent experiencing one of the "special stories" anglers sometimes tell about night fishing. And, oh yeah, one more thing, anyone who has ever night-fished and tells you it doesn't cause any anxiety probably hasn't done that much of it.

How and What To Try First

One of the first things to remember about night fishing is you can use any fly you would normally use during the day. While you do not need the full selection of flies day-time angling requires all the flies you normally use will produce at night. With one notable exception (a Harvey "pusher" fly) the best pattern to try first is something which imitates what the browns are currently feeding on. The good news is the size of the pattern can be increased dramatically with no ill effects, and the pattern does not have to be an exact imitation—just close.

Study what the insect activity, if any, has been like during the day. During the dog days of summer certain hatches can get started at dusk and really get rolling after dark. Many, many nights caddis hatches after nightfall have yielded some tremendous brown trout angling. I have also fished a (somewhat rare) cranefly hatch well into the night, as well. If practical, always try to start with a surface fly. Carefully drifting a surface fly over an area creates very little disturbance and still leaves nymph and streamer patterns as an option. Obviously if you've been catching fish all week during the day on Muddler Minnows don't hesitate to lead off with one, but your chances with a surface fly after dredging the area with a streamer are greatly diminished. Most of the time you find browns most active during the first three hours after it gets dark. Usually a nymph or a surface fly will serve you best for the first two of these hours, and it is best to finish the last hour with a streamer.

Let's assume, for the sake of argument, it is a typical late, hot summer evening. You arrive at the spot you want to fish in plenty of time to watch darkness cover it. Your eyes have adjusted, you're seeing pretty well and you are ready to start casting. Before it got dark you took two really nice browns on a #14 Elk Hair Caddis. The browns are still feeding on them. Instead of staying with the #14, go ahead, change flies and put on a #12 at the minimum and more likely a #10. Since we already have the fly off the end of the line let's eliminate the 5X tippet you were using before nightfall and go up to a 3X or a 2X. Now you are ready to begin your first cast to the areas which have been dark the longest.

Earlier insect activity has determined the fly choice. Increasing the size of the fly has helped in several ways. As odd as this may sound, on all but the darkest nights there will be some visibility. You may not be able to see your fly at all times but you'll be amazed how often you can follow its wake. This holds true, especially on the flat, slower water. If you would like even more visual contact with your fly, tie some of your flies with the black post-wing covered in the previous chapter. Larger fly size will not only render a higher hook-up per strike ratio, but because of the larger hook gape it will also help you hold larger fish. Tying the fly to a larger diameter tippet aids with this as well.

If the dry fly doesn't produce, the next best bet would be a fly designed to sit in the water's surface film. A perfect example of this is the Partridge and Peacock soft hackle mentioned earlier. Almost any pattern tied "wet fly style" on a nymph hook is an excellent choice. Make sure to spin the hackle on any flies tied for this purpose extra "leggy"; a few extra turns will do nothing but bolster the flies effectiveness.

Nymphs and streamers are subject to the same rules. Extra turns of hackle or even doubling up on feathers will create the appearance of a larger fly while not reducing hooking capabilities. Allow some variance in the amount of lead you apply per fly. I like to use a lighter fly at night than I do during the day. In this particular situation you are actually trying to get a bad drift. As a matter of fact the more wake the fly creates the better you're going to do. This brings us to presentation.

Presentation

For all the time devoted to proper presentation in the earlier chapters this will pale in comparison. Down and across is the only way to consistently present the fly in the dark. For a detailed description of this presentation go back to Chapter 5. It causes the fly to leave a wake which grabs the brown's attention. Brown trout lose many of their daytime inhibitions and don't hesitate to follow a fly dragging on the surface. Another advantage to this cast is it's simple. Remember it is dark while you're making the cast and the drift, it is almost guaranteed anything more complicated than this will end up in a monumental tangle. If you raise and miss a brown with this presentation quickly try another cast and mend upstream to slow the fly's drag, there is a very good chance the same brown will try another take.

The only other night presentation technique is applicable only to streamers while they are being fished down and across. This involves a "pumping" method taught to me by some hard-core European sea trout anglers. After you make the downstream cast, and before the current begins to carry the line across, grab the fly line between the reel and the first stripping guide. Quickly pull this line in and then let it go back out. Repeat this as the streamer swings across the current. When the fly has completed the swing don't pull it out right away for another cast.

Slowly continue the pumping motion five or six times. Let the fly rest a while longer and then pick it out of the water for another cast. Don't ask me to explain it but this technique seems to work very well. Try it the next time you are fishing a streamer at night.

Equipment

You will be glad to know along with presentation simplicity comes equipment simplicity. All of the recommended gear in the previous chapters will be, if anything, too much gear to use at night. After dark, fancy contraptions and gadgets will do nothing but cause you to spend time fiddling with them instead of fishing. Besides, nobody else can see you anyway. Instead of specialized equipment, night fishing demands familiarity so be sure to take gear you use regularly and trust.

Aside from familiarity be sure the rod and reel you choose is about one line size greater than what you think you will need. If you feel you can get by with a six weight—don't, take a seven. Earlier it was mentioned not to worry about fishing the same area during the day you wish to fish at night because it was probably a different group of browns using the spot. Well, they're also probably a larger group of browns. Go prepared for bigger fish.

If you really feel you have to have some specialized equipment and are planning on spending some serious night fishing hours, I would abandon the idea of the traditional fly vest. They are hard enough to find your way around when it's light. Instead try one of the many chest packs that are available. These are much smaller and keep everything out in front of you where you can easily see it with your light.

Lights for night fishing are something you will purchase, evaluate, change, quit using, mess with, discard and pick up and try again. The more night fishing you do the more serious the search for the perfect light will become.

As I write this, I glance around the room and count about a dozen lights, which at their time of initial purchase were intended for streamside use after dark. The earliest lights are a direct reflection of my budget during the early years. Not much was asked of them. As a matter of fact, the measurement of a good light then was simply whether or not the damn thing would work the entire evening without having to be beat against a tree. The next stage followed the "bigger is better" philosophy. Problem here was they were so big you ended up constantly having to set it down anytime you wanted to do anything other than use the light, and they require an entire hand just to carry them.

Technology has finally advanced to the point a small lightweight flashlight mounted on a headband is now the only thing used. Recently somebody told me they were originally manufactured and marketed to backpackers. This light is both reliable and durable it has the added quality of being about four times as bright as any light I have ever owned. The headband leaves both hands free for tying on flies, landing and releasing fish, etc... Now if only someone would invent a way to turn this light on and off while your hands are full or down at your side, it would be about perfect.

If you talk to other night fishermen invariably the finer points of light use will arise. Red colored light is supposed to spook less trout than a direct bright light. This is one of the great debates among those who pursue browns after dark. Of the few folks I have encountered while night fishing, about half of them were using either a light with a red lens or had their regular flashlight lens covered with a piece of red kitchen shrink wrap. Most of these gentlemen seemed to know what they were doing, but in all honesty did not seem to be hooking-up any more browns than those who had nothing covering their lights. Does it matter? I am not sure. The few times I have tried covering the lens with a red wrap, it reduced the light's effectiveness

Fish the shallow areas which go dark first.

A high-quality reel can enhance your nymph fishing. This brown was feeding on midge larvae.

to the point I was unable to see where I was going and I did not catch any more than on average; I abandoned this technique. Now I try to use the light only for walking from one run to another, changing flies or adding new tippet.

Another helpful hint regarding light use involves landing a fish. Once you hook a brown and are successful bringing him to hand it is a good idea to leave your light off until the fish is in the net. Obviously, it is sometimes too dark to do this, but if there is any natural light at all, try to get the fish in the net before turning on your light. Otherwise you will have a very difficult time even getting close; the larger the brown the harder they will fight once they see the light.

Safety

Night fishing is without a doubt the most dangerous of all the angling techniques. A few common sense safety measures can keep a fun time from turning into a possible life threatening one. A good first step is to always go with a partner. The better you know this person and their abilities the more comfortable you will be. If this is not an option, the smallest safety precaution you should take is telling someone where you are going. This way, on the outside chance a search has to be initiated, people will at least have an idea of where to begin. Another question I am constantly being asked is about

the safety of wading belts. This surprises me. Very intelligent people still believe in the old wives tale... "if you fall in while wearing chest waders (sans a wading belt) the water will rush into the waders and pull you under and you will drown." This is simply not true. Water inside your waders will equalize with the water in the river or lake you happen to be in, and as a result it will not pull you under. Now if you try to stand up, all the water that is inside your waders you have now just brought higher than the water on the outside and it will try to pull you back down. In short: Gravity works! So what is the best solution if you fall in? Stay on your back with your legs in front to keep you off the larger rocks and your arms spread to either side for stability and then make your way to quiet water on the edge. Once here simply roll over and crawl out.

Do I wear a wading belt? Yes, most of the time, but not for any reason that has to do with safety. I wear one because it keeps my waders pulled in and pulled up—it is simply more comfortable.

Night fishing can be very enjoyable when done correctly and safely. If the first several times out fail to yield something do not give up—keep trying! As crowded as the rivers are becoming, if you are ever going to catch the brown trout of your life this will more than likely be the technique.

CHAPTER EIGHT

FLIES FOR BROWN TROUT

If there is one item in the equipment of fly fishermen that is truly magical it would have to be the fly. There is not a single aspect of tying trout flies I don't enjoy. It is very surprising how relaxing it can be. President Carter once told me he used to unwind from a day of Presidential duties by tying (while listening to Willie Nelson) a few dry flies.

One of the few things that bothers me about fly patterns is the lack of attribution, or, probably more specifically, the lack of attempt. For all of the patterns listed I have tried to make sure the originators and tiers received their due. If any have been passed over, it was not my intention. On the other hand, I have unmercifully tweaked the original materials and tying order.

When it comes to constructing flies for brown trout I am a slave to durability. Unfortunately, most flies being produced fail to meet this requirement. There are plenty of ways to combat this, but it would be a little outside the focus of this book. Maybe a tying book will be next?

Give these patterns a look. Most are simple to build and all of them work! As I was choosing the patterns, I noticed there was not a single one that has failed to prove itself. There are no "one time wonders" included. They were weeded out a long time ago.

Nymphs

Anderson's Brown Stone

Hook: Nymph, 3X long, size 8 to 12
Thread: Brown or tan, unwaxed
Tail: White rubber legs
Abdomen: Dark brown and tan yarn, woven so the brown is on top and the tan underneath
Legs: White rubber legs
Thorax: Hare's ear fur spun in a dubbing loop and picked out

Bighorn Shrimp

Hook: Nymph, 1X long, size 10 to 16
Thread: Tan, unwaxed
Underbody: A layer of tan tying thread
Body: A combination of seal's fur substitute, comprised of 1/3 brown, 1/3 pink, 1/3 orange; spun in a dubbing loop and picked out
Shellback: Closely trim body material on top and sides of fly
Rib: Copper wire

Bitch Creek

Hook: Nymph, 2X long, size 4 to 12
Thread: Black, unwaxed
Tail: Black rubber legs
Abdomen: Woven black and orange ultra-chenille
Thorax: Black ultra-chenille
Legs: Two brown hackles palmered through thorax
Antennae: Black rubber legs
  Notes: *Tying the antennae back over the body makes this fly easier to tie on*

Box Canyon Stone

Hook: Nymph, 2X long, size 4 to 12
Thread: Black, unwaxed
Tail: Dark brown goose biots
Abdomen: Black yarn twisted and wrapped tightly to look segmented
Thorax: Wrapped black yarn
Legs: Two brown hackles palmered through thorax
Wingcase: Dark brown turkey coated with head cement

Brassie

Hook: Nymph, size 12 to 18
Thread: Black, unwaxed
Abdomen: Copper wire
Head: Black dubbing or peacock herl

Nymphs

Anderson's Brown Stone

Bighorn Shrimp

Bitch Creek

Box Canyon Stone

Brassie

Flashback Hare's Ear

Flashback Pheasant Tail Nymph

Freeman's Crystal Scud

Gold Ribbed Hare's Ear Nymph

Innis' Amberstone

LaFontaine's Deep Sparkle Pupa

Mathews' Serendipity

Mathews' Serendipity (Bead-Head)

Mercer's Z-Wing Caddis

Montana Damsel

Mosquito/Midge Larva

Palamino Midge

Peacock/Red Butt Soft Hackle

Pheasant Tail Nymph

Prince Nymph

Bead-Head Prince Nymph

San Juan Worm

Sexton's Moose Mane

Troth Stonefly

Whitlock's Red Squirrel Nymph

Flashback Hare's Ear

Hook: Nymph, 1X to 3x long, size 6 to 18
Thread: Tan, unwaxed
Tail: Hare's mask fibers/guard hair
Abdomen: Dubbed hare's ear and mask hairs
Rib: Copper wire
Thorax: Same as abdomen except applied in a dubbing loop
Wingcase: Pearl Krystal Flash

Flashback Pheasant Tail Nymph

Hook: Nymph, 1X stout, size 12 to 18
Thread: Brown, unwaxed
Tail: Pheasant tail barbs
Abdomen: Same as tail except wrapped
Rib: Fine copper wire
Thorax: Same as abdomen
Wingcase: Pearl Krystal Flash pulled over thorax

Freeman's Crystal Scud

Hook: Standard nymph, size 12 to 18
Thread: Light tan, unwaxed
Body and Rib: Tan Antron mixed with gray sparkle yarn spun in a dubbing loop constructed of several strands of Krystal Flash
Shellback: Trim body closely on tops and sides
Originated by David Freeman, this fly is an excellent spring creek pattern

Hare's Ear Nymph

Hook: Nymph, 1X to 3X long, size 6 to 18
Thread: Tan, unwaxed
Tail: Hare's mask fibers/guard hair
Abdomen: Dubbed hare's ear and mask hairs
Rib: Copper wire
Thorax: Same as abdomen except applied in a dubbing loop
Wingcase: Dark turkey coated with head cement
Notes: *Experience has shown the wingcase can be eliminated or replaced by trimming this area very closely*

Innis' Amberstone

Hook: Nymph, 1X long, size 10 to 12
Thread: Black unwaxed
Tail: Black goose biots
Rib: Medium gold wire
Body: Amber dubbing comprised of two parts yellow rabbit, one part rust rabbit, and 1/2 part orange rabbit
Gills: Black ostrich herl
Legs: Black goose biots
Originated and tied by Mark Innis

LaFontaine's Deep Sparkle Pupa

Hook: Nymph, 1X stout, size 12 to 16
Thread: Light tan unwaxed
Underbody: Green dubbing
Overbody: Mixed light brown and creme Antron body wool tied in at the bend, separated and pulled forward to form a bubble around the underbody
Legs: Lemon dyed wood duck
Head: Natural muskrat, dubbed
Notes: *This is an excellent pattern. The above recipe is not original, but one I have altered. Check out Gary's book Caddisflies*

Mathews' Serendipity

Hook: Curved nymph, size 14 to 18
Thread: Tan, unwaxed
Body: Olive, red, or creme Z-Lon, segmented
Head: 6-7 strands of deer hair clipped short

Mercer's Z-Wing Caddis

Hook: Nymph, 1X stout, size 12 to 16
Thread: Light tan, unwaxed
Abdomen: Olive dubbing
Rib: Copper wire
Wing: Creme/Ginger Z-Lon
Head: Peacock herl

Montana Damsel

Hook: Nymph, 1X to 3X long, size 6 to 12
Thread: Light or dark olive, unwaxed
Tail: Light green marabou tied short
Abdomen: Two to three strands of light green ostrich herl, trimmed short after wrapping
Rib: Small copper wire
Thorax: Same as abdomen, but not clipped
Wingcase: Light turkey coated with head cement

Mosquito/Midge Larva

Hook: Nymph, 2X long, size 14 to 18
Thread: Brown, unwaxed
Tail: Natural mallard flank
Abdomen: Stripped peacock herl
Rib: .007" diameter clear mono
Thorax: Peacock herl
Antennae: Natural mallard flank tied back

Palamino Midge

Hook: Nymph, 1X short(or curved), size 14 to 18
Thread: Tan, unwaxed
Abdomen: Extended gray or brown ultra chenille or new dub singed on the end
Thorax: Natural muskrat dubbing
Wingcase: Tan Antron body wool

Peacock/Red Butt Soft Hackle

Hook: Dry fly, size 12 to 18
Thread: Brown, unwaxed
Tail: Red yarn, tied short
Body: Peacock herl, twisted and wrapped
Rib: 4X clear mono
Hackle: Hungarian partridge or bobwhite quail breast feather

Pheasant Tail Nymph

Hook: Nymph, 1X stout, size 12 to 18
Thread: Brown, unwaxed

Tail: Pheasant tail barbs
Abdomen: Same as tail except wrapped
Rib: Fine copper wire
Thorax: Same as abdomen
Wingcase: Pheasant tail barbs pulled over thorax

Prince Nymph

Hook: Nymph, 1X long, size 10 to 14
Thread: Black, unwaxed
Tail: Dark brown goose biots
Body: Peacock herl, twisted and wrapped
Rib: Copper wire
Horns: White goose biots
Collar: Brown hackle

San Juan Worm

Hook: Nymph, 1X long, size 8 to 12
Thread: Red, unwaxed
Underbody: Red vernille, singed on the ends
Overbody: Red Larva Lace or Swannundaze
  Notes: *This pattern has been attributed to many, but the originator is Mr. Paul Pacheco, a middle school principal from Shiprock, New Mexico*

Sexton's Moose Mane

Hook: Nymph, 1X stout, size 14 to 18
Thread: Tan, unwaxed
Tail: Natural mallard flank
Underbody: Tan, unwaxed, tying thread
Abdomen: Wrapped ivory ends of moose mane, (or creme Antron body wool, which is a little more durable)
Rib: .007" dimeter clear mono
Thorax: Peacock herl
Wingcase: Dark turkey coated with head cement
  Originated by Dale Sexton, this fly is almost unstoppable on spring creeks

Troth Stonefly

Hook: Nymph, 6X long, size 2 to 6
Thread: Black, unwaxed
Tail: Black rubber legs
Underbody: Black chenille, wrapped tapered
Legs: Black rubber legs
Overbody: Mixed black and brown seal fur substitute, spun in a dubbing loop and trimmed on top and bottom
Antennae: Black rubber legs
  Tied by J.M. Conley

Whitlock's Red Squirrel Nymph

Hook: Nymph, 1X long, size 8 to 16
Thread: Tan, unwaxed
Tail: Stacked red squirrel tail fibers
Abdomen: Red squirrel underbody mixed with a light tan Antron
Rib: Heavy copper wire
Thorax: Dubbed red squirrel back hair
Legs: Mottled hen hackle
  Notes: *Experience has shown the legs of this pattern are probably not necessary*

Dry Flies

Baetis Compara-Dun

Hook: Standard dry fly, size 12 to 18
Thread: Olive, unwaxed
Tail: Brown Z-Lon (trailing shuck)
Body: Olive dubbing
Wing: Natural elk hair tied in a 180 degree arc over top of the hook

Black Foam Ant

Hook: Standard dry fly, size 12 to 16
Thread: Black, unwaxed
Abdomen: Black closed cell foam
Legs: Black hackle
Thorax: Black closed cell foam

Black Herl Midge

Hook: Standard dry fly, size 14 to 18
Thread Black, unwaxed
Tail: Black hackle barbs
Body: Black ostrich herl
Rib: 6X, clear monofilament

Compara-Emerger

Hook: Standard dry fly, size 6 to 16
Thread: Tan, unwaxed
Tail: Moose mane fibers, divided
Body: Grayish-tan dubbing
Wing: Elk hair
Head: Butt ends of wing trimmed short

Conley's Blue Wing Olive Parachute

Hook: Standard dry fly, size 14 to 18
Thread: Olive, unwaxed
Wing: Orange Antron body wool
Body: Olive dubbing
Hackle: Grizzly, tied parachute style

Conley's Hi Viz MacSalmon

Hook: Dry fly long, size 2
Thread: Orange, unwaxed, and black, unwaxed
Body: Orange macrame; threaded and extended, with the end burned closed
Underwing: Mottled fly sheet; tied tent style
Wing: Light elk
Overwing: Fluorescent pink Antron body wool
Head and Collar: Chocolate elk hair, spun and trimmed
  Tied by J.M. Conley

Everybody's Low Water Caddis

Hook: Standard dry fly, size 10 to 16
Thread: Tan, unwaxed
Wing: Natural elk hair
Hackle: Brown
Antennae: Stripped brown hackle stems
  Notes: *This Larry Duckwall pattern seems to work best when it is tied as sparse as possible*

Dry Flies

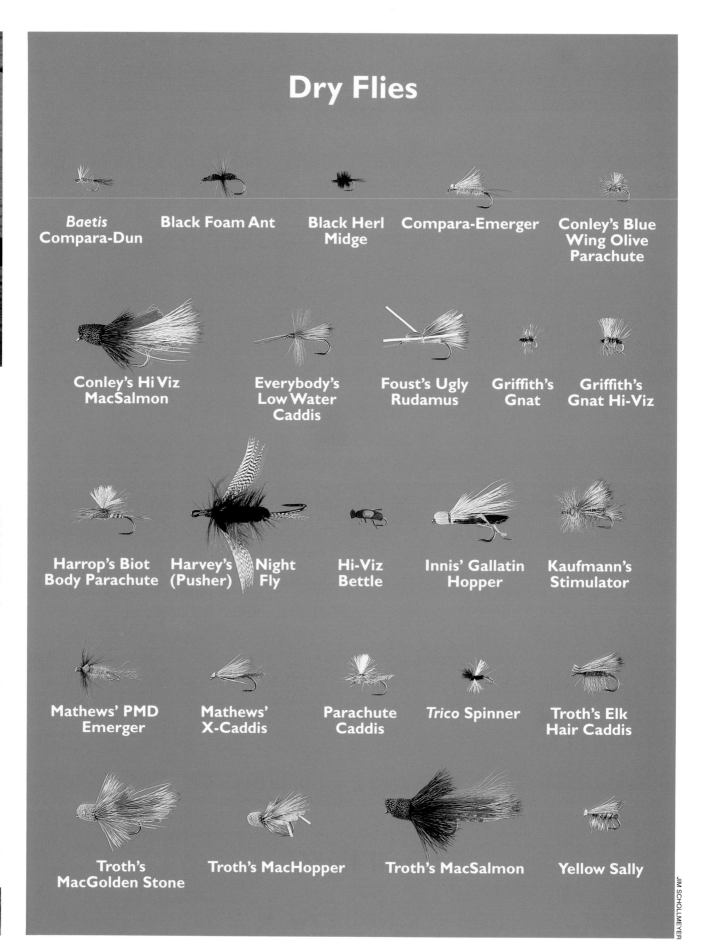

Baetis Compara-Dun   **Black Foam Ant**   **Black Herl Midge**   **Compara-Emerger**   **Conley's Blue Wing Olive Parachute**

Conley's Hi Viz MacSalmon   **Everybody's Low Water Caddis**   **Foust's Ugly Rudamus**   **Griffith's Gnat**   **Griffith's Gnat Hi-Viz**

Harrop's Biot Body Parachute   **Harvey's (Pusher) Night Fly**   **Hi-Viz Bettle**   **Innis' Gallatin Hopper**   **Kaufmann's Stimulator**

Mathews' PMD Emerger   **Mathews' X-Caddis**   **Parachute Caddis**   **_Trico_ Spinner**   **Troth's Elk Hair Caddis**

Troth's MacGolden Stone   **Troth's MacHopper**   **Troth's MacSalmon**   **Yellow Sally**

Foust's Ugly Rudamus

Hook: Standard dry fly, size 6 to 14
Thread: Yellow, unwaxed
Tail: Natural elk hair
Body: Flashabou; front 1/3 yellow thread
Head and Wing: Elk hair pulled back bullet-head style, over the top half only
Legs: Round white rubber legs

Griffith's Gnat

Hook: Standard dry fly, size 14 to 18
Thread: Black unwaxed
Body: Peacock herl
Hackle: Grizzly; palmered
Rib: 6X, clear mono

Griffith's Gnat Hi-Viz

Hook: Standard dry fly, size 14 to 18
Thread: Black unwaxed
Post: Orange (or black) Antron body wool
Body: Peacock herl
Hackle: Grizzly; palmered
Rib: 6X, clear mono

Harrop's Biot Body Parachute

Hook: Tiemco model 100, sizes 10 to 14
Thread: Olive, unwaxed
Tail: Bright yellow grizzly hackle fibers
Abdomen: Canada goose biot, dyed to match tail
Thorax: Rusty olive dubbing
Wing: Dark dun turkey biot
Hackle: Bright yellow grizzly hackle
Tied by Arco Iris Flies

Harvey's Night (Pusher) Fly

Hook: Dry fly, size 4 to 2/0
Thread: Black, unwaxed
Tail: Natural teal flank fibers
Underbody: Black closed cell foam; tapered
Body: Black poly dubbing
Hackle: Black; matched pair; palmered
Wings: Quilled teal breast feathers; lacquered with head cement

Hi-Viz Bettle

Hook: Standard dry fly, size 14 to 18
Thread: Black, unwaxed
Legs: Black bettle leg material
Body: Black closed cell foam with a dot of orange lacquer
Head: Same as body except trimmed in front of hook eye
Tied by Orvis Company

Innis' Gallatin Hopper

Hook: Dry fly 2X long, size 6 to 12
Thread: Olive, unwaxed
Body: Olive deer hair tied surrounding the hook shank, and then ribbed with tying thread
Underwing: Natural deer hair

Wing: Mottled turkey, tied tent style
Overwing: Yellow elk hair
Legs: Dyed yellow grizzly hackle stems; knotted to form joint
Head and Collar: Natural elk tied bullethead style, and secured with orange thread
Originated and tied by Mark Innis

Kaufmann's Stimulator

Hook: Dry fly, 3X long, size 6 to 14
Thread: Orange, unwaxed
Tail: Elk tied "hard", so it flares
Abdomen: Olive dubbing
Body Hackle: Brown; palmered
Rib: Fine gold wire
Wing: Elk, flared wide
Thorax: Orange dubbing
Front Hackle: Grizzly
Tied by Arco-Iris Flies

Mathews' PMD Emerger

Hook: Standard dry fly, size 12 to 16
Thread: Brown, unwaxed
Tail: Brown Antron body wool or Z-Lon
Body: Yellowish-tan dubbing
Wing: Gray closed cell foam
Legs: Several turns of dun

Mathews' X-Caddis

Hook: Standard dry fly, size 12 to 18
Thread: Tan, unwaxed
Tail: Brown Antron body wool or Z-Lon
Body: Olive dubbing
Wing: Elk hair

Parachute Caddis

Hook: Standard dry fly, size 10 to 16
Thread: Tan, unwaxed
Post Wing: White poly or Antron body wool
Body: Tan dubbing
Overwing: Mottled fly sheet; tied tent style
Hackle: Grizzly

Trico Spinner

Hook: Standard dry fly ring-eye, size 14 to 18
Thread: Black, unwaxed
Tail: White hackle; stripped and divided
Body: Black poly dubbing
Wing: White Antron body wool
Post Wing: Black Antron body wool
Head: Black dubbing

Troth's Elk Hair Caddis

Hook: Standard dry fly, size 10 to 16
Thread: Tan, unwaxed
Body: Tan (or any other color) dubbing
Hackle: Brown; palmered through body
Rib: Fine gold wire
Wing: Natural elk hair

Notes: This Al Troth pattern is quite possibly the best western dry fly pattern ever created

Troth's MacGolden Stone

Hook: Dry fly long, size 6
Thread: Gold, unwaxed
Body: Gold macrame; threaded and extended, with the end burned closed
Underwing: Mottled fly sheet, tent style
Wing: Elk, dyed olive
Overwing: Fluorescent pink Antron body wool
Head and Collar: Olive elk hair; spun and trimmed
Tied by J.M. Conley

Troth's MacHopper

Hook: Dry fly long, size 8 to 10
Thread: Gold, unwaxed
Body: Yellow macrame; threaded and extended, with the end burned closed
Legs: Yellow rubber legs (flat)
Underwing: Mottled fly sheet; tied tent style
Overwing: Bright yellow elk hair
Head and Collar: Yellow elk hair; spun and trimmed
Tied by J.M. Conley

Troth's MacSalmon

Hook: Dry fly long, size 2
Thread: Orange, unwaxed, and black, unwaxed
Body: Orange macrame; threaded and extended, with the end burned closed
Underwing: Mottled fly sheet; tied tent style
Overwing: Light elk
Head and Collar: Chocolate elk hair, spun and trimmed
Tied by J.M. Conley. MacSalmons flies Mike has tied have appeared in several books with other people claiming to have tied them, this is the first time he has been given due credit. I don't think there is anyone better at spinning and trimming hair

Yellow Sally

Hook: Standard dry fly, size 14 to 16
Thread: Yellow unwaxed
Tail: Red yarn
Body: Yellow floss
Body Hackle: Yellow floss
Wing: Elk hair
Head: Butt ends of wing clipped short
Tied by Mark Bauman

Streamers

Black/Green Yuk Bug

Hook: Streamer, 3X long, size 2 to 8
Thread: Black, unwaxed
Tail: Gray squirrel with Krystal Flash
Legs: White rubber legs
Body: Black or green chenille
Hackle: Grizzly; palmered
Rib: Clear mono

Blue (Black) Electric Bugger

Hook: Streamer, 3X long, size 2 to 8
Thread: Black, unwaxed
Tail: Black marabou and a few strands of blue Flashabou
Body: Black chenille with tail pieces of blue Flashabou pulled forward
Hackle: Black
Head: Black chenille
Rib: Clear mono

Blue Smolt

Hook: Streamer, 3X long, size 2 to 8
Thread: Black, unwaxed
Body: Silver Mylar; secured with fluorescent orange thread
Tail: Unraveled Mylar
Throat: Red bucktail
Wing: Blue bucktail under a flat mallard flank feather

Bow River Bugger (3 styles)

Hook: Streamer, 3X long, size 2 to 8
Thread: Black, unwaxed
Tail: Black marabou
Body: Dark olive chenille
Rib: Fine copper wire
Hackle: Olive or brown
Head and Collar: Dark elk, spun and trimmed
Tied by J.M. Conley (all three styles)

Cactus Bugger

Hook: Streamer, 3X long, size 2 to 8
Thread: Tan, unwaxed
Tail: Black marabou and pearl Krystal Flash
Body: Peacock crystal chenille
Hackle: Black
Rib: Clear mono

Dark Spruce

Hook: Streamer, 3X long, size 2 to 8
Thread: Black, unwaxed
Tail: Peacock sword
Body: Red floss and peacock herl
Rib: Copper wire
Wing: Dark furnace hackles; curving out
Collar: Dark furnace hackle

Dennis' Kiwi Muddler

Hook: Streamer, 3X long, size 2 to 8
Thread: Black, unwaxed
Tail: Unraveled pearlescent Mylar
Body: Pearlescent Mylar secured with white thread
Wing: White rabbit strip and a few strands of pearl Flashabou
Head and Collar: Natural deer hair; spun and trimmed
Tied by Dan Bailey Flies

Egg Sucking Leech

Hook: Streamer, 3X long, size 2 to 8
Thread: Black, unwaxed

Streamers I

Black Yuk Bug

Blue (Black) Electric Bugger

Blue Smolt

Bow River Bugger (three styles)

`Cactus Bugger

Dark Spruce

Dennis' Kiwi Muddler

Egg Sucking Leech

Francis' Crayfish

Fire-tail Woolly Bugger

JIM SCHOLLMEYER

Streamers II

Green/Black Electric Bugger

Green Yuk Bug

Girdle Bug

Muddler Minnow

Picket Pin

Red-Belly Girdle Bug

Red-Belly Yuk Bug

Troth Bullhead

White Marabou Muddler

Wool-Headed Sculpin

Zonker

JIM SCHOLLMEYER

Tail: Black, unwaxed
Body: Black chenille
Hackle: Black
Rib: Clear mono
Head: Chartreuse green chenille

Fire-tail Woolly Bugger

Hook: Streamer, 3X long, size 2 to 8
Thread: Black, unwaxed
Tail: Red marabou and Krystal Flash over brown marabou
Body: Brown chenille
Hackle: Furnace
Rib: Clear mono

Francis' Crayfish

Hook: Streamer, 3x long, size 2 to 8
Thread: Black, unwaxed
Pincers: Two bunches of red squirrel tail; divided
Body: Dark brown chenille
Legs: Black hackle; palmered
Rib: Clear mono
Tail: Lacquered hen feather tied in upside down
  Notes: *Although I have changed some parts of this fly and "adopt-ed" it, the original idea for this fly started out as a Dennis Kavanaugh pattern he calls the Vibrator*

Green/Black Electric Bugger

Hook: Streamer, 3X long, size 2 to 8
Thread: Black, unwaxed
Tail: Black marabou and a few strands of green Flashabou
Body: Black chenille with tail pieces of green Flashabou pulled forward
Hackle: Black
Head: Black chenille
Rib: Clear mono

Girdle Bug

Hook: Streamer, 3X long, size 2 to 8
Thread: Black, unwaxed
Tail: White rubber legs; divided
Legs: Two or three pair of white rubber legs
Body: Black chenille

Muddler Minnow

Hook: Streamer, 3X long, size 2 to 8
Thread: White, unwaxed
Tail: Mottled turkey
Body: Gold tinsel
Wing: Gray squirrel under mottled turkey wing quills
Head and Collar: Natural elk; spun and trimmed
  Tied by J.M. Conley

Picket Pin

Hook: Streamer, size 2 to 8
Thread: Black, unwaxed
Tail: Red squirrel tail
Body: Peacock herl
Hackle: Brown hackle; palmered over body

Rib: Clear mono
Wing: Gray squirrel tail
Head: Peacock herl

Red-Belly Girdle Bug

Hook: Streamer, 3X long, size 2 to 8
Thread: Black, unwaxed
Legs: Two pair of white rubber legs
Body: Black chenille
Underbody: Piece of fluorescent red chenille tied-in lengthwise
Rib: Clear mono

Red-Belly Yuk Bug

Hook: Streamer, 3X long, size 2 to 8
Thread: Black, unwaxed
Tail: Gray squirrel tail with Krystal Flash
Legs: White rubber legs
Body: Black chenille with a single strand of fluorescent red chenille pulled underneath and forward
Hackle: Grizzly palmered
Rib: Clear mono

Troth Bullhead

Hook: Salmon up eye, size 1/0 to 6
Thread: Black, unwaxed
Tail: Black marabou and peacock herl
Body: Creme yarn
Throat: Red yarn or dubbing
Back: Black marabou and peacock herl, pulled forward from the tail
Head and Collar: Dark elk; spun and trimmed

White Marabou Muddler

Hook: Streamer, 3X long; size 2 to 8
Thread: White, unwaxed
Tail: Red hackle barbs
Body: Silver chenille
Wing: Peacock herl over white marabou
Head and Collar: Light elk; spun and trimmed

Wool-Headed Sculpin

Hook: Streamer, 3X long, size 2 to 8
Thread: Black, unwaxed
Tail: Black marabou and a few strands of pearl Krystal Flash
Body: Dark green or black chenille
Hackle: Black palmered over entire body
Head: Dark green or black wool; spun and clipped

Zonker

Hook: Streamer, size 2 to 8
Thread: Black and red
Body: Pearlescent Mylar folded over aluminum gutter tape
Tail: Unraveled Mylar
Hackle: Red
Wing: White rabbit strip
  Tied by Arco-Iris Flies

CHAPTER NINE

ODDS AND ENDS

This chapter, simply by virtue of being last, is really nothing more than some left-overs. By this I don't mean items which were not good enough for the other chapters, but rather things which didn't fit. These are the type of left-overs you really look forward to the next day. There might be a tip or two which will make some aspect of your fishing a little easier or more productive.

Politics of Place

Brown trout anglers are currently faced with a problem that was virtually unknown twenty years ago. There is almost too much information on where to go. There are magazines, videos, newsletters and even seminars on good places to fish for browns. Recently I even saw an advertisement for a computer service. For a monthly fee jumping brown trout and a current list of "hot spots" will appear on the screen of your computer. While this information can be helpful, it has created an angling mind-set equivalent to a salad bar. Fly fishermen now seem to judge a successful fishing holiday by how many different pieces of water they can fish in a week's time. While this is all in good fun, the fly fisherman seeking brown trout needs to stay more focused. Cutthroat, rainbow and brook trout can be fished for, browns must be hunted. One of the best ways to accomplish this is by using local knowledge.

A gentleman talking about the three rules of success for the restaurant business once said, "location, location, location." Successful brown trout fishing is dependent on this same axiom. An excellent brown trout spot is worth its weight in gold and is usually protected accordingly. These places are occasionally stumbled onto, but are usually a product of local knowledge. This does not necessarily mean fishing one river for thirty years until you recognize every rock, nor does it mean you must hire a local guide everywhere you go. Those are just two ways local knowledge can be obtained.

Having local knowledge gives you the ability to pursue, recognize, obtain and fish well, places with high brown trout populations and minimal angling pressure during the times you are there. Successful brown trout angling requires you apply yourself. Find out where that "good size creek running under the road" originates—is it privately owned? Will the landowner let you fish? Instead of floating the river with the crowds between 8:30 a.m. and 4:30 p.m., why not float from 12:00 p.m. to 8:00 p.m.? Ask

Penka River in Russia.

Good brown trout water is guarded accordingly.

the guy behind the counter selling you flies where he fishes on his day off. And if you are lucky enough to find out—go! Many times I've seen this actually happen only to have the fisherman who asked turn to his buddy and say, "Oohh boy, that's over an hours drive one way. If we go there we'll never make our 5:30 dinner reservation. You got any place closer?"

One of my favorite ways to obtain local knowledge is the often talked about, but seldom used method of asking patrons in the local bar. Many years ago, David Freeman and I spent a very sunny, very unproductive day floating the Jefferson River. As anybody who as ever fished this river can tell you, on a bright day you would swear there isn't a fish in it. If it is overcast the browns can be so cooperative the end of the day finds you babbling like an infant. We finished the float and proceeded to one of the local watering holes. The only other person in the place besides the bartender, was an older gentleman who appeared to have been there for quite some time. When we sat down with our beers he started to warm up a little.

"Boys been on the river?"

"Yeah, it was pretty slow. Too bright."

He turned on his bar-stool and said, "Too bright my ass. You boys want to catch some fish?"

We purchased a beer for our new friend. He bummed a quarter, headed for the pay phone and soon returned with permission and directions. If you have ever received directions in a bar to a secret trout hole you know how quickly they can become epic. We were also hurried by the fact that only two hours remained before sundown. Luck was on our side. The directions were simple, and we

soon found ourselves delightfully isolated at what used to be an old fish hatchery. A small spring creek, which originally provided the water for the operation, had slowly reclaimed the gravel raceways. What was left was a pretty substantial pond with a constant supply of fresh spring creek nutrients. Almost as if on cue, large brown trout were rising to Blue-winged Olives. In the remaining purplish light of the day we caught and released large brown trout as quickly as our tiny dry flies and delicate tippets allowed. On the way home we swore each other to secrecy and vowed never to return without the other. It has been difficult, but so far I have upheld my end of the agreement.

As more fly fishermen hit the streams in search of brown trout these places are becoming increasingly difficult to obtain. This brings up an often unspoken code among ardent brown trout fishermen. If you are lucky enough to have somebody show you a special brown trout spot, it will come with some responsibilities. First and foremost don't tell anyone else without prior approval; not even someone you are related to. Secondly it is in very poor taste to return to that spot without the person who originally showed it to you. At the very least you should have that person's prior blessing. I've seen some long-time angling relationships become destroyed over this very issue. While responsibility is on the recipient's end, the benefactor also needs to be reasonable. If your friend's "special spot" is a float trip from the after-bay access to the 13 mile access on the Bighorn River or a spring creek that charges $50 per day, waiting for an invitation to return would be absurd. If the special spot involves a private landowner I'd check first. This system really works well for several reasons. It creates incentive for everybody to find

Try to wear an earth-tone
shirt when angling.

catch him or not will depend on how well you use your new-found experience and knowledge.

The take-home lesson is that local knowledge, regardless of how you obtain it, is worth the effort. Local knowledge is one of the greatest (and most often overlooked) tools the brown trout angler has. Not only will it reward you with places to apply your skill but it will also bring more brown trout to hand once you are there.

Clothing and Gear Tips

It is amazing the number of anglers who show up for a guided trip with all the best gear, but they are wearing a bright white or red shirt. Always try to wear an earth colored shirt or even a camouflaged one—you will catch more browns.

▲

I once guided for three months alongside a guide from New Zealand. I learned quite a bit, but one of the neat things he taught me was to use a woman's nylon stocking for tailing fish. Once the stocking is wet, pull it over your hand and simply grab the fish. The small mesh netting gives you a non-slip grip and does not injure the fish.

▲

If you do any traveling with your fly gear duct tape is invaluable. I've tried about every kind of security tactic

their own special place to fish—a show me your's and I'll show you mine type of thing. Good places not only produce good fishing but can then be used as trading stock to access other good spots.

Landowners are more comfortable when they know at least one person in a party. Anglers who can't keep their mouths shut usually only find out about one or two marginal places to fish before the word gets out they are not to be trusted. Never take an unknown fishing partner to your best place on your first trip together. Try him out on one of your less important places first.

Occasionally local knowledge can be bypassed if you don't mind paying to fish. So called trespassing fees are now being charged to access privately owned brown trout streams. Most of these streams can have wonderful fishing. Fees can range anywhere from $25 to $100 per day depending on the stream's popularity. Are they worth it? It depends. Ask to take a quick look at the stream before handing over your money. If stream banks and the riparian zone are cattle trampled, exposing soil which has caused knee-deep sediment in an overly widened channel, the answer is no. If the owner has fenced these areas off and seems to be taking care of the stream then it is probably worth forking over the cash. If the owner is realizing a revenue from the stream it only stands to reason the resource should be well taken care of and a quality product offered.

Local knowledge as it pertains to fishing simply means being astute and learning from experience. The number of fly fishermen who don't do this would astound you. There is nothing wrong with making a tactical wading mistake on a large rising brown trout—once. Providing he doesn't get pressured too much, he will be there at the same time, doing the same thing tomorrow. Whether you

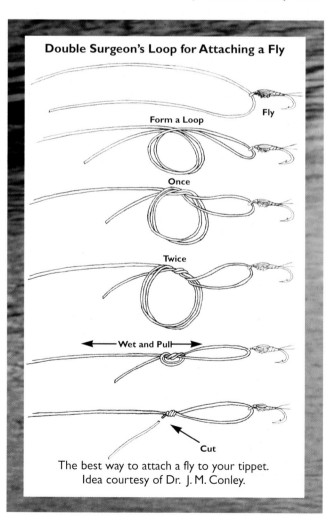

Double Surgeon's Loop for Attaching a Fly

Fly

Form a Loop

Once

Twice

◄—Wet and Pull—►

Cut

The best way to attach a fly to your tippet.
Idea courtesy of Dr. J. M. Conley.

Catch and release, done properly, will ensure our sport will be around for future generations.

known to man—a some have worked, some have cost me gear. Let's face it, the only thing in the world which works like a rod duffel or tube is a rod duffel or tube. By wrapping lids, zippers, locks and any other points of entry with copious amounts of duct tape, it makes getting into them too big a hassle, and the airline crooks won't have time to fool with it. This has been the only method which has worked 100 percent over the years.

▲

Whoever first decided to use spun and clipped deer hair for the heads on streamers, kind of missed the boat. It works well and is durable enough, but deer hair floats and streamers are supposed to sink. A quick way to alleviate this problem is to carry a small bottle of biodegradable dish soap with you. Soak the deer hair heads with the soap immediately after tying them on. This helps water saturate the hair faster and improves the sinking qualities of this material. The smell of this does not bother the fish.

▲

Forget about every knot you have ever used to attach a fly to your tippet. The double surgeon's loop is the only knot you should use for this task. Mike Conley, once again, deserves credit for figuring this one out. This has been tested around the world on many different species for about seven or eight years, and I will stake my reputation on it. There is not a better knot for this! It is quick, easy, can be done in the dark, provides increased action to the fly, and is stronger than any other knot ever used to attach fly to tippet. Play with the knot according to the diagram. Smaller loops will be a result of practice.

▲

When you purchase a new pair of wading boots have a new set of felt pads installed. Put the new felt on top of the felt which is already on the boots. This will make your boots last twice as long. The stitches and the sides will wear out long before the felt. Another wading boot trick is to purchase a length of small diameter rock climbing rope at the nearest outdoor store and use it for your laces. The stuff is usually colored a little funky, but it will not come untied and is very durable.

▲

Secure all the items you use regularly to the outside of your vest with old fly line. This includes line snips, fly floatant, hook hone, etc... Tie these items on so you have enough extra line to move these things around as you use them. Avoid zingers, I've never seen one which continued to work for any length of time.

▲

Tuck away a small set of fly tying scissors in your vest. You will find they are indispensable for trimming marabou tails and making minor adjustments to the hackle on dry flies.

▲

Avoid the use of droppers when you are experimenting with different types of nymph rigs. I have never seen any which eventually didn't end in a tangled mess. If you use one nymph, and present it correctly to the right places, you will catch just as many browns as if you were using two flies at once.

▲

Make a habit of cleaning your fly line(s) more often than you do. A good product for this is Armor-All plastic protectant. A clean line not only lasts longer but also clears the guides easier.

This is also a good product for cleaning graphite rods, and will help improve your casting. If you don't have any Armor-All any quality car wax will also work well on your favorite rod.

▲

Another safety tip for those who chase their brown trout close to town—be mindful of overhead power lines. Not many people realize it, but graphite fly rods are excellent conductors of electricity. Add this to the fact you are usually waist deep in water when you are using one and these can make a deadly combination.

▲

Catch and Release

It has become fashionable to put a catch and release section in every fly fishing book. For this reason I almost did not put one in. Not until last summer anyway. For some unexplainable reason I witnessed more fly fishermen doing strange things while releasing fish than ever before. As a result here it is again: 1)Play the fish quickly, don't drain it of every last drop of energy. 2)Always try to land the fish while you are in at least knee deep water. Dragging a trout onto a gravel bar will eventually kill that fish, as will kicking a fish to shore. 3) If you don't want a photograph there is no reason to touch the trout; simply reach down and pull the hook out.

As you can see from the previous pages I love to take, and look at, fish photographs. If you do want a photograph have the camera ready to go and then briefly lift the fish out of the water for the picture. Quickly return the fish to water and then rest the fish in some quiet side water until it can leave your hand under its own power.

Studies have proven if you release a fish within 70 yards of where you caught its, chances of survivability increase dramatically. As brown trout anglers we have many responsibilities, but always making sure there are brown trout around to fish for should be primary—lest we lose them, we have lost it all.

BIBLIOGRAPHY

"A Fish Exhibition." New York Times, March 29, 1881: page 8 (col. 3).

Bachman, R. A., Behavior of Free-Ranging Wild Brown Trout In A Stream. Doctoral Thesis (Pennsylvania State University). University Park, Pennsylvania. 1982.

Bashline, Jim, Night Fishing For Trout. Wautoma, Wisconsin: Willow Creek Press. Reprint, 1987. New York: Dell Publishing.

Brown, C.J.D., Fishes of Montana, Bozeman, Montana: Big Sky Books (Montana State University). 1971.

Courtenay, Walter R. Jr., Jay R. Stauffer Jr., Distribution, Biology, and Management of Exotic Fishes. Baltimore: The Johns Hopkins University Press, 1984.

Edwards, T.L., Captain, E. Horsfall Turner, The Angler's Cast. London: Herbert Jenkins, 1960.

"Fish Eggs For Germany." New York Times. December 21, 1880: page 1 (col. 3).

Harvey, George, Techniques of Trout Fishing and Fly Tying. Belleville, Pennsylvania: Metz Hatchery. 1985.

Hatch, Michael, James E. Sublette, Mary Sublette, The Fishes of New Mexico. Albuquerque, New Mexico: University of New Mexico Press, 1990.

Heacox, Cecil E., The Compleat Brown Trout. New York: Winchester Press, 1977.

Henkin, Harmon, Fly Tackle. New York: J.B. Lippincott, 1976.

Jennings, Preston, A Book of Trout Flies, New York: Derrydale Press. Reprint. 1970. New York: Crown.

LaFontaine, Gary, Trout Flies, Proven Patterns, Helena, Montana: Greycliff Publishing Co., 1993.

_____. Caddisflies. Piscataway, New Jersey; New Century Publishers, 1981.

_____. The Dry Fly, New Angles, Helena, Montana: Greycliff Publishing Co., 1990.

Leonard, Edson, R., Flies. New York: Barnes & Co., 1950.

Lutton, John, R., "The First Introductions of Brown Trout, Salmo Trutta, In the United States." Fisheries. Vol. 20, no. 1. (1985): 10-13.

MacDonald Rose, M. E., An Analytical Subject Bibliography of the Publications of the Bureau of Fisheries 1871-1920. Doc 899. Washington: Government Printing Office, 1921.

Marinaro, Vincent, In the Ring of the Rise. New York: Crown Publishers, 1976.

Mather, Fred, "Brown Trout In America." Bulletin of the United States Fish Commission Vol. VII. No. 136. (1887): 21.

_____. Modern Fishculture In Fresh and Saltwater. New York: Forest & Stream Publishing Co., 1900.

Merwin, John, et. al.. Stillwater Trout. New York: Nick Lyons Books, 1980.

Norris, Thaddeus, American Fish Culture. Philadelphia: Porter & Coates, 1868.

_____. American Anglers Book. Philadelphia: Butler Publishing, 1864.

"Progress of Fish Culture." New York Times, January 12, 1882: page 6 (col. 4).

Ramsbottom, Robert, The Salmon and its Artificial Propagation. London, England: Simpkin Marshall & Co., 1854.

Schullery, Paul, American Fly Fishing, A History. New York: Nick Lyons Books, 1987.

Schwiebert, Ernest, Trout. New York: Dutton, 1978.

Skues, G.E.M., Minor Tactics of the Chalk Stream. London: Black, 1924.

"State Fisheries Interests." New York Times. January 12, 1882: page 6 (col. 4).

Stewart, Dick, Farrow Allen, Flies For Trout. North Conway, New Hampshire: Mountain Pond Publishing, 1993.

"The Werra's Quick Passage." New York Times. February 24, 1883: page 8 (col. 5).

INDEX